Cooking WITH for Kids

Kirly-Sue

First published in 2019
by The Stanborough Press Ltd.
Alma Park, Grantham, Lincolnshire, UK.

British Library Cataloguing in Publication Data.
A catalogue record for this book
is available from the British Library.

ISBN: 978-1-78665-954-5

Designed by Abigail Murphy.

Printed in Serbia.

Introduction

Vegan cooking for children is easier than you think! In this book you will find simple and easy-to-follow recipes, using ingredients that are easy to find and are probably in your kitchen cupboard already.

Making fresh, delicious vegan meals for and with your child has many benefits. I have two nieces and one nephew. I remember when my eldest niece was about 7 years old and she was staying with me for the day during the school holidays. She seemed a little bored, so I asked her if she would like do some cooking with me in the kitchen. Before I could even finish the sentence she rushed to the bathroom to wash her hands, ran back in record time and said, 'I'm ready now.' Bless her; she was so eager, and it's quite a nice thing to do that can be quite bonding too.

My nephew loves cooking and is very good in the kitchen; he has also been interested in plants since he was about 8 years old. He now grows his own vegetables and tropical fruits in his greenhouse. He is a keen gardener like my dad. My youngest niece baked cookies with me once when she was smaller, and we decorated them with some lettering that said, 'God Is Love'. She was helping me to make them for the children at my local church. I always make cookies for them when it is my turn to take the children's class.

I have always done some kind of cooking or baking with my nieces and nephew, so I have learnt first-hand about the different kinds of things children like to eat, and also the things they like to cook and bake.

Many parents want to give their children vegan meals (some regularly and some occasionally). I have been a vegan for many years, and many of the viewers of my TV show and YouTube channel are parents. I get many questions about suitable dishes to serve to children, and also recipes that children can make with a little help from a parent or guardian.

Try not to feel too nervous about experimenting with some of the ingredients or adding a few more herbs and spices, if required. Just relax and try again if you don't get it right the first time around. No one gets it right all the time; I have made many cooking and baking mistakes, and I have learnt that it takes practice, prayer and a little confidence.

Kirly-Sue

 You Tube Kirly Sue   🐦 @KirlySuesKitchen

 Kirly-Sue's Kitchen   @KirlySuesKitchen

Why Become a Vegan?

Once you've established a healthy lifestyle, you may be delighted to know that this may be your best 'diet' – not a fast for you – great for slimming down, and energising, as it is a low-calorie and low-fat diet. Contrary to the unhealthy fad diets, which usually leave you feeling tired and usually leave you putting the weight you lost back on, going vegan is the healthy way to keep the extra fat off for good, while leaving you with plenty of energy.

Do you love those cute animals advertised on television that are being rescued by the RSPCA and other animal welfare societies? Then the next level of support you can give is to become a vegan. Assuming animals were not killed every time we stopped eating meat, did you know that being vegan saves 198 animals a year?

Rather than restricting your diet as a vegan, there are so many different substitutes and alternatives that you as a vegan can eat – much more than you could possibly imagine! You can find a lot of sites on veganism and recipes by referring to my recipe book, but there are also many other varieties, cuisines and flavours of vegan recipes. So you're worried that if you become a vegan you'll have to give up chicken curry, cheese sandwiches, and ice cream? Don't be, as the demand for vegan foods is soaring (you're not on your own), and so the food industries are introducing more delicious and tasty meals and desserts.

According to the Academy of Nutrition and Dietetics, vegans are less likely to develop heart disease, cancer, diabetes, or high blood pressure than meat-eaters are. Vegans get all the nutrients that they need to be healthy in avocados, nuts, seeds, olive oil and so on.

Eating meat doesn't just hurt animals: it restricts the amount of food on the planet for people, especially deprived people. It takes tons of agriculture and water to farm animals for meat. In fact, it takes up to 6kg of grain/grass to produce only 450g of animal meat! All that plant food could be used much more effectively and efficiently if it were fed directly to people. The more people who go vegan, the better able we'll be to feed the hungry.

Consuming meat is wasteful in terms of energy transfer; it also causes enormous amounts of pollution, and the meat industry is one of the biggest causes of climate change. Adopting a vegan diet is more effective than switching to an eco-friendly electric car in the fight against climate change.

Food Allergies & Sensitivities

Allergies are becoming much more common. According to the *World Allergy Organisation Journal*, worldwide there are at least 200 to 250 million who experience food allergies. As a loving parent or guardian, you will naturally be anxious to know if your children are likely to have an allergic reaction to a given type of food, and you will be sure to use caution when introducing a new food to your child for the first time, even if other members of your household have found it to be harmless.

An allergy is a hypersensitivity of the immune system to a foreign substance, such as pollen, house dust or particular foods, which are harmless to non-allergic people. The over-reactive immune system treats these normally harmless substances as invaders, going into emergency mode with the well-known allergic responses of wheezing (asthma), running nose (allergic rhinitis or hay fever), and skin problems (eczema, urticaria or nettle rash) and, in extreme cases, anaphylactic shock – a very dangerous, potentially fatal condition. Some people have a much greater tendency to these reactions than others, and their condition is known as atopy. Most cases of atopy involve many factors, including foods, but the term 'food allergy' is also used very widely for all sorts of reactions to foods, many of which are not allergies at all. For these the term 'food sensitivity' is better.

Both true food allergies and other food sensitivities are much more common now than they were twenty or thirty years ago. This is especially so with nut allergy, particularly peanut allergy, where a potentially fatal reaction to this normally harmless legume can come on within minutes. Unfortunately such severe reactions are much more common than they were.

Why is this so? Many people now have unstable immune systems that overreact, like a burglar alarm set to call the police when burglars enter, but which in fact goes off when a spider walks past. Instead of producing a few drops of fluid to flush out some pollen grains, these over-reactive immune systems produce a torrent of hay fever or a severe attack of wheezing. Research is needed to find out why so many people's immune systems are so sensitive. Theories range from immune system overload due to the vast number of foreign chemicals to which we are exposed now, to immune system underactivity due to our over-hygienic environment. Another possible cause is that immunisation programmes have wiped out the childhood illnesses that helped to build healthy immune responses in the past. Probably all these factors play a part, but the fact is that we don't really know.

Although we do not fully understand food allergies and sensitivities, we do know that improving general health, lifestyle and environment can greatly diminish, if not actually completely eliminate, many of these problems. It is a little-known fact that asthmatics and other atopic sufferers can be helped very much by changing their diet. The same is true for those who find that specific food sensitivities cause problems as diverse as digestive upsets, sinusitis, chronic fatigue, nerve-related conditions and even arthritis.

Frequently-used foods are the most likely culprits – such well-trusted staples as milk, bread, chocolate and even orange juice. In the West most people have grown up to look on milk as almost the ideal form of nutrition, but it can cause major problems. Actually, as many as 90% of adults worldwide lack the enzymes needed to digest cow's milk. Milk production methods have also changed a lot in recent decades, as has the food industry. With milk in some form added to almost every processed food you can imagine, many people are getting milk overload. Milk sensitivity contributes to the truly allergic (atopic) problems and also to many ear, nose and throat conditions, as well as a great many bowel disorders. Another problem food seems to be wheat. It is another frequently eaten food and many people now eat less of other cereals, such as oats, rye, barley, or rice, to balance it. It's as if the body finally gets wheat overload and goes on strike. There are now very few varieties of wheat grown, and this may well add to the problems. It's interesting that in the UK around one in every hundred people suffer from coeliac disease and have a severe gluten (wheat protein) intolerance, but many more people than that are buying expensive gluten-free products. Most of these people seem to have jumped on the gluten-free bandwagon, because they think they may be intolerant or as a precaution in case they might be. A good plan would be for them to look very carefully at their whole lifestyle as well as their diet, because there could be many other reasons for their problems.

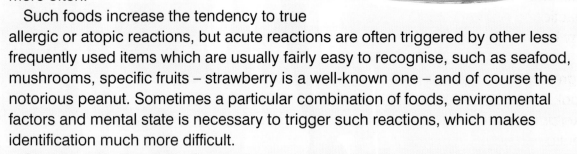

Another problem group is the methyl xanthenes – they're in tea, coffee, chocolate and cola – another type of substance that many people use daily or more often.

Such foods increase the tendency to true allergic or atopic reactions, but acute reactions are often triggered by other less frequently used items which are usually fairly easy to recognise, such as seafood, mushrooms, specific fruits – strawberry is a well-known one – and of course the notorious peanut. Sometimes a particular combination of foods, environmental factors and mental state is necessary to trigger such reactions, which makes identification much more difficult.

So what does this mean for you and your children? Those who have experienced severe reactions should of course be under medical care, avoid the obvious causes and have medication for emergency use. They should continue this regime but also start lifestyle programmes to stabilise and strengthen their immune systems. Such programmes include exercise and stress control as well as a healthy diet. Those with less serious problems will benefit from such programmes too, and it's well worth trying a simple elimination diet to find out what their main triggers are.

As milk is the most common problem food, the first step would be to eliminate it and all its by-products as completely as possible from the diet, preferably for a few weeks. If that works, try a 'challenge' – a serving of dairy produce. If the sneezing, bowel cramps or other symptoms recur, the best plan is to avoid all dairy produce for two or three months. After that, many people find they can tolerate it occasionally, sometimes even regularly. The same can be done with wheat, methyl xanthenes and other foods you suspect of causing mild problems. If you are really keen, you can try eliminating dairy, wheat, chocolate, and so on, all at the same time, and then reintroduce them gradually, one by one, to see which ones cause problems. Please take great caution if your child is known to be at risk of suffering a potentially life-threatening reaction such as anaphylactic shock in response to a particular food, however. That food should be avoided by the child as much as possible.

Eliminating irritating foods is not the whole story, however. They need to be replaced by a wide variety of whole and healthy foods. Base your diet around unrefined starches; add plenty of fruits and vegetables, and smaller helpings of foods made from beans, nuts (if you're not allergic to them) and seeds. Eat a wide variety of foods from day to day, but a small variety at any one meal. Avoid eating between meals or late at night. Exercise is very important too, as is avoiding poisons. Cultivating a peaceful and contented frame of mind may be the most important remedy of all.

It goes without saying (but we'll say it anyway!) that if you suspect your child to be at risk of suffering from an allergic reaction in response to any of the ingredients, or combination of ingredients, in this book, then please exercise the utmost caution when preparing your food. Although all the ingredients used in this book will be completely harmless and indeed beneficial to most people, please be cautious if your child has not encountered one of them before, and especially if your child has previously suffered an adverse reaction to one of them. Use your God-given wisdom and parental instincts. Neither the author nor the publisher will be held liable if you fail to do this. Show your children how to prepare food safely and wisely, and have a great time cooking with them!

How to Become a Vegan

So what does it mean to be vegan?

Veganism is a subset of vegetarianism. There are several different types. Some vegetarians still drink milk and/or eat eggs: not vegans. They are the strictest vegetarians and don't make allowance for *any* animal products in their diet. It is by far the most challenging form of vegetarianism, because people take a lot of things for granted. Eggs and milk, for example, are common baking ingredients; so substitutions need to be made if a vegan is going to be able to eat baked goods.

What makes food vegan, or not?

In order for food to be strictly vegan, it needs to adhere to certain criteria. It is important to note that there are a lot of hidden ingredients in foods. It is especially important to watch out for these if you are going to strive for a vegan diet.

- Vegans don't eat animal products or by-products of animal products.
- That means that they don't consume things like milk and eggs.
- Vegans also don't eat fish.
- Don't forget that bees are an animal, so vegans also don't eat honey, royal jelly, or bee pollen supplements.
- There are also plenty of hidden ingredients to look out for that tend to make their way into food, including gelatin, lard, and whey.

If you are a new vegan, making all of these changes may seem overwhelming; but, after you've been eating and cooking the vegan way for a while, you will become an old pro.

Things to consider and where to start

There are vegans everywhere. Unfortunately, you can't spot them on the street and ask them what the best way for them to approach veganism was. However, along the lines of alternatives and substitutes you can surf for communities online or look for a local club or group in your area. The easiest way to do this is to find a new favourite vegan restaurant, a favourite table, and go from there. The Vegan Society has a great website that's full of resources and news, and even helps you shop!

Just to help you start, here's a balanced vegan menu for the day:

Breakfast:

Oatmeal with nuts and dried fruit (most commercial oatmeal is vegan) • Fresh fruit

Lunch:

Avocado Reuben • Sumptuous spinach salad with orange-sesame dressing

Dinner:

Tofu-spinach lasagne • Fresh tossed salad

You don't have to be a nutritionist or medical doctor to understand the background of healthful living. Learning as much as you can about nutrition, food and health will only do you good. You'll become an expert in no time when it comes to plant-based alternatives. You'll still get your protein if you know what to look for. Luckily, plenty of plants are high in it: tofu, beans, nuts, seeds, quinoa and wholegrains are all protein-packers.

Get a physical

Take your medical history into account. For example, those with anaemia or osteoporosis need to take extra care to make sure they have sufficient iron and calcium intake, as well as keeping a balanced diet.

Science of veganism

Soon you'll become an expert in plant-based alternatives.

Top tips

Pace yourself

Make minor changes to your diet throughout your transition until you've reached your end goal.

Be the right vegan

Although vegans have a low-calorie and low-fat diet, they may not have a healthy lifestyle yet: it needs to be well rounded and include a wide variety of nutritious foods.

Shop around

Experiment with new tasty vegan foods to step outside your comfort zone. There are probably more alternatives than you think.

Learn on the go

Have a positive attitude to your new lifestyle, and have the courage to undertake new challenges.

Seek advice

The internet is now a great source of information with so many vegan groups and forums to explore for help.

Remind yourself why you're a vegan

When you have a bad food day, watch uplifting veganism videos or look at shocking statistics about meat consumption.

Keep moving forwards

There is always a greater reason to keep up with your decision instead of abandoning it. Take it one meal at a time. Vegan living will soon become second nature.

Substitutions

Butter
- Coconut oil
- Vegetable oil
- Plant-based butter alternatives

Cheese
- Tofu cheese
- Nutritional yeast
- Cashew cheese
- Potato and carrot cheese

Egg
- Apple sauce
- Bananas
- Ready-made egg replacers
- Aquafaba – chickpea brine
- Water and ground chia or flax seeds (flegg)

Milk
- Coconut milk
- Soya milk
- Hemp milk
- Rice milk
- Almond milk
- Cashew milk

Honey
- Agave nectar
- Maple syrup
- Coconut nectar

Meat
- Tempeh
- Seitan
- Beans & pulses
- Aubergine (eggplant)
- Mushrooms
- Jackfruit

Replacing milk in recipes

Vegans don't consume milk from any animal (sheep, cow, goat, and so on). Milk is a very common ingredient when baking and cooking. It is much easier to replace than eggs. To replace milk in recipes, just substitute any of these vegan alternatives. For example, if the recipe calls for one cup of milk, use one cup of soya milk instead. Here are some alternative milk options:

Soya milk

Soya milk comes in a variety of flavours and is readily available in many supermarkets. Flavours include vanilla, unsweetened, chocolate, and even strawberry. Some brands are thicker and creamier than others. You may need to do some experimenting before you find the brands you like the best. Soya milk is usually a fairly neutral flavour and blends well in most recipes. Soya milk is also rich in protein.

Nut milks

Nut milk beverages such as almond milk and hazelnut milk are also good options. Unlike soya milk, these nut milks have a distinct flavour and may not work well in every recipe. They are usually available in sweetened and unsweetened varieties as well.

Rice milk

Rice milk is also a great option to replace milk in recipes. It is also very mild-tasting and blends well in most recipes. However, it is important to note that rice milk typically doesn't contain a lot of protein, so you may need to compensate for that during the day.

As you become familiar with the different flavours of non-dairy milk replacement products, you'll start to get a feel for which recipes will taste best with them.

Replacing buttermilk in recipes

Buttermilk is also an important ingredient used in several different recipes. For a vegan, using traditional buttermilk is impossible since it is an animal product. Buttermilk is simply regular milk that has been cultured, which means that it has some good bacteria in it, much like yoghurt.

Luckily, you can easily make your own. The process is as follows. It makes one cup of vegan-friendly 'buttermilk'.

1 Measure one cup of **soya milk** in a glass measuring cup.

2 Add 1 tablespoon of **vinegar** or **lemon juice** and mix.

3 Let it sit for about fifteen minutes before using it.

There are several different things you can use to replace buttermilk, but soya milk works the best. Rice milk and nut milks don't work as well; soya milk works much better.

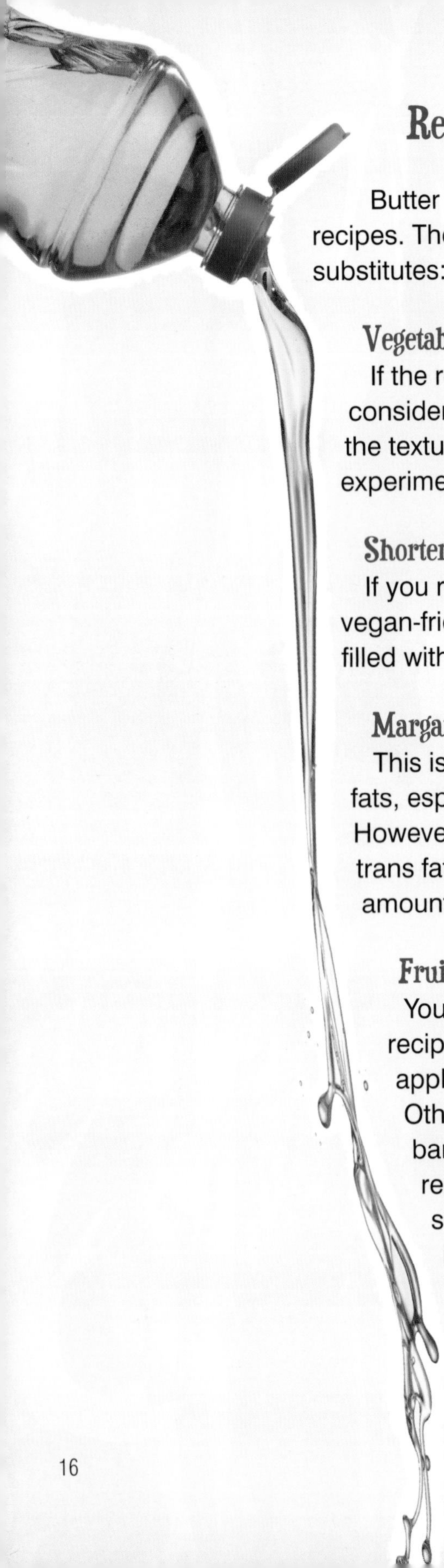

Replacing butter and lard in recipes

Butter is another important ingredient used in a lot of recipes. There are several different things you can use as substitutes:

Vegetable oil

If the recipe calls for melted or even solid butter, you can consider using vegetable oil instead. This, however, may alter the texture of the recipe a little, so you will probably need to experiment.

Shortening

If you really need a solid fat to use in recipes you can use vegan-friendly shortening. This is a manufactured product and filled with trans fats, so using it in moderation is best.

Margarine

This is another option that can replace butter or other solid fats, especially if you want something with a buttery flavour. However, margarine is also high in trans fatty acids. Watch for trans fat-free products, but even those may contain trace amounts of trans fats.

Fruit purée

You can reduce fat with fruit purées. For example, if the recipe calls for 1 cup of butter, you can try using ½ cup apple sauce and ½ cup vegan margarine or shortening. Other fruit purées you can use include plum purée and banana purée. You may be able to find fruit purée fat-replacement products in the supermarket. Just make sure they are vegan-friendly and that you follow the instructions for making a proper substitution.

Always make sure that the butter replacement products are used in moderation. A diet that is high in fats and trans fats is not a healthy diet. If you absolutely need them, just use them once in a while.

Replacing eggs in recipes

As much as we'd like to avoid using eggs in our vegan recipes, it can be a challenge. In fact, this is one of the most difficult ingredients to replace. However, there are many options to choose from that will get the job done.

What do eggs do in the recipe?

In certain recipes, eggs are almost essential: they bind ingredients together. They can be used to make baked goods rise and they also help make them light and fluffy. Eggs also help the product form some structure and also provide extra moisture. They are especially useful while baking and particularly for certain savoury dishes as well.

Egg replacement options

Here is a list of some of the best egg-replacement options out there. You can replace the eggs in any recipe using these options.

Puréed bananas

Puréed bananas are an effective egg substitute. Just place a peeled banana in the blender and pulse until completely smooth and without any lumps. Half a regular-sized banana is the equivalent of one egg.

The positive aspect of using bananas is that they are readily available. However, bananas have a distinct taste that won't work out in every recipe. For example, if you were trying to make peanut butter cookies, the banana flavour would alter the taste.

Ground flaxseeds

It is best to purchase the flaxseeds whole and store them in the refrigerator. When it's time to use them, measure out 1 tablespoon of flaxseeds for every egg that you need to replace; then pulverise them in a blender or coffee grinder.

Transfer the flaxseeds to a bowl and add three tablespoons of water for each egg you need to replace. Add the water slowly while whisking vigorously. Whisk until the mixture has a gel-like consistency.

Since flaxseeds are nutty-tasting, this egg replacement works best when making things like wholegrain breads, muffins, and pancakes. You may want to experiment to get a feel for the types of recipes you like this to be in.

Egg-replacement products

There are several egg-replacement products on the market that are designed to be vegan-friendly. Look at the packaging to make sure that it's vegan-safe and that it doesn't contain any meat by-products.

These egg-replacement powders get mixed reviews. Some people like them a lot; others don't. They're definitely convenient and good to have on hand. Once you get used to cooking vegan, you'll start to learn which foods taste best using egg-replacement products.

Since there are several brands on the market, it may take a while to find one that you're happiest with. When using these, just follow the package instructions. They usually come in powder form. If you can't get them at the health food store, you can easily get them online.

Tofu

Tofu is also another option you can try if you need to find a replacement product. You can try any form of tofu, but this may take some experimentation. Silken tofu seems to yield the best results. You can also use plain soya yoghurt in the same proportion with similar results.

The nice thing about tofu is that it blends well with most flavours. Tofu doesn't have a lot of flavour on its own, especially when paired with stronger ingredients. Another advantage is that it is widely available in most areas, and in most supermarkets.

To use, just take the tofu and blend it until smooth in the blender. A food processor works well, but it's important to make sure that there are no lumps and the texture is as smooth as possible. To replace one large egg, use ¼ cup of the blended mixture.

You'll need to do some experimenting to see which recipes work best with tofu as an egg substitute. It all depends on the kinds of recipes you try and your personal preferences.

Flour and other raising agents

You can also use pastes made from different kinds of flours and raising agents to replace the eggs. The benefit is that most homes have these ingredients on hand. They also don't have flavour. They can be blended into the batter fairly easily.

It may take some experimentation to get the proportions right. Here are some options:

- 1 tablespoon flour of any kind (try wheat flour, oat flour, or soya flour) and 1 tablespoon water for each egg.
- 1 tablespoon baking powder, 1 tablespoon flour, 2 tablespoons water for each egg.
- 2 tablespoons corn starch and 2 tablespoons water blended together also replaces one egg.

Finding the right egg substitute

Again, as you try these different combinations, you'll get a feel for which egg substitutes work best for which recipes. As a suggestion, you may want to start with one of your favourite foods and try different egg substitutes until the flavour and texture you desire are reached.

For example, if you want to make a batch of blueberry muffins, you can substitute the eggs with any one of these substitution options. Make a note of how it tastes. Next time you make it, try another egg substitute. After trying several, think about which one was your favourite, and you will soon be able to tell at a glance which egg-replacement products work best for certain kinds of recipes.

Common Ingredients

Vegan cooking is certainly an art. Ingredients such as milk, buttermilk, eggs, and butter are almost essential for certain recipes: but, as we explored, the substitutions are more than adequate. With that said, there are a lot of ingredients that a lot of vegan chefs find essential. Here's a rundown of some of the most common.

Soya products

Soya is probably the most versatile plant out there, especially when it comes to creating healthy and protein-rich vegan meals. Here is a list of some of the soya products that are out there:

Soya milk

This is readily available and can be found in several different flavours, such as vanilla and chocolate.

Tofu

Tofu comes in different levels of firmness, such as extra firm or soft.

Tempeh

Tempeh is a fermented product with a hearty, meaty texture that can be used in stir-fries and other meals.

Ground meat replacement

This soya food is a staple to some, because you can make meals such as spaghetti bolognese and vegan chilli.

Soya yoghurt

This contains the active cultures, just like regular yoghurt, and comes in a variety of flavours.

Miso

Miso is a fermented salty paste that is made from soya and is used as a popular, enzyme-rich soup base.

Tamari and soy sauce

Both condiments are made from soya.

Edamame

These are the fresh soya beans and are excellent by themselves or in stir-fries.

Vegan cheese

Vegan cheese even melts and has a similar texture to real cheese.

Soya sausage, hot dogs, and hamburger patties

Vegans can enjoy breakfast sausages, hot dogs, and even hamburger patties!

There is a variety of soya products out there, and this isn't a complete list. It just illustrates the variety of the food products. Look for soya products that are made from non-genetically modified soya beans.

Soya foods have their critics. Some only like to use them in their 'traditional' forms, such as tofu, tempeh, miso, edamame, and tamari. Opponents of processed soya products are wary of the fact that they are designed to taste like meat or milk products, which, to them, defeats the purpose of being vegan. Plus, these foods tend to be highly processed, which doesn't necessarily make them healthier. Whether or not you decide to use them is a decision that you should make after you weigh up the pros and cons.

Wholegrains

There are so many different kinds of wholegrains out there; it is worthwhile to experiment. Grains are rich in vitamins, minerals, fibre and other important nutrients. They have protein, especially quinoa – an ancient grain that is especially protein-rich. Here are some wholegrain products to try:

- Rye
- Buckwheat
- Quinoa
- Wheat products
- Pasta
- Brown rice
- Oats

These can be ground into flour or used whole. They can form the backbone of a healthy vegan diet.

Nuts and seeds

These are another essential part of a healthy vegan diet. They are rich in vitamins and minerals, as well as important nutrients like healthy fats. Here's a list of some nuts and seeds to try:

- Hazelnuts
- Walnuts
- Sunflower seeds
- Pumpkin seeds
- Pecans
- Almonds
- Cashews
- Sesame seeds
- Poppy seeds
- Flax seeds
- Hemp seeds

You can include them in recipes and also eat them by themselves as a snack.

Legumes (beans & pulses)

Legumes are an essential protein source to a vegan, especially when paired with wholegrains. They need to be combined in this way in order to form a complete protein. When this is one of your main protein sources, it is important to remember to combine it.

Here are some examples. This list is by no means exhaustive:

- Chickpeas (garbanzo beans)
- Kidney beans (red peas)
- Black beans
- Cannellini beans
- Northern beans
- Black-eyed peas
- Split peas
- Gungo peas
- Butter beans
- Red lentils
- Green lentils
- Puy lentils

You can find legumes in a dried form, ground into flour, and canned. The dried form needs to be soaked overnight in order to soften it. The canned form is easy to use and great to have on hand. The flour is also a popular ingredient in baked foods and savoury cooking.

Fruits and vegetables

Important for good health, fruits and vegetables add colour and variety to your meals. As a vegan, your entire diet will be plant-based, so you need to get your vitamins, minerals, and nutrients from things like fruits and vegetables.

Look for organic produce whenever possible, which is even healthier. Organic food is also better for the environment. Seasonal, local produce is also best, because it helps support your local economy and tastes a lot fresher.

Canned and packaged foods

As the vegan diet increases in popularity, so does the availability of packaged, vegan-friendly foods. What follows is a list of some of the things you can find.

- Breads
- Desserts
- Baked goods
- Snacks
- Vegan chocolate
- Canned goods
- Beverages
- Breakfast foods and cereals
- Sausages
- Burgers
- Mince
- Ready meals (Like macaroni cheese & burritos)
- Pies

The great thing is that you don't even need to go to a health food store to find a lot of these products. Yes, health food stores have a lot of vegan options, but you can even find vegan products in your regular supermarket.

Setting up your vegan pantry

Setting up your pantry is an essential step to being able to create meals easily. For people who have been vegetarians all their lives, setting up the pantry will not be a struggle. However, if you've just recently become a vegan, you'll probably need to start from scratch. You may have some ingredients on hand, but most of your pantry may not be vegan-friendly.

Of course, this list will not include perishable items such as fruits and vegetables. However, even some perishable items, such as certain brands of tofu, soya milk, rice milk, almond milk, and so on, can be stored on the shelves and not in the refrigerator because of their special packaging.

Step 1: take inventory

The first step to building a vegan pantry is to take inventory of what you have. This step is mostly for those who have just become vegans. However, if you have been vegan for a while, you will also benefit from this. The goal is to go through and think about everything that you have and determine whether it supports the vegan lifestyle.

You may also want to look at the ingredients lists of all your packaged foods to determine whether any of the hidden ingredients listed in the previous chapter exist. Even if you have been vegan for a while, you may still find some foods in your pantry that you should not have there.

If you do find a lot of foods to get rid of and they have not been opened, do not throw them away. Give them away to a local food bank. Just because you will not eat them does not mean that someone will not benefit from them and appreciate having something to eat.

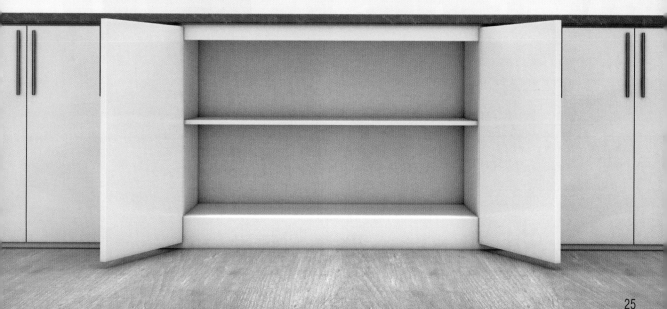

Step 2: stock the essentials

It isn't entirely necessary to have a large pantry filled with tons of ingredients and packaged foods. All you need to do is sit and think about the things that are really important to you. If you don't bake that often, for example, don't bother buying baking supplies until you really need them. If you are the type of person who loves cereal and has a few bowls a day, you may want to keep packages of nut milk, soy milk, rice milk, and extra cereal in your pantry so you don't need to run to the store all the time.

Once you figure out what you need and what your eating preferences are, you can start buying things to put in your pantry. If you do not take the extra time to think about what you need, you'll end up purchasing things you won't eat. Then the food will go to waste. Just stock the essentials, and if you need other things then you can buy them as you go along.

Step 3: purchase any extras

It can be expensive to stock your larder all at once. There are certain ingredients that you may need once in a while, such as tomato sauce and other items. It isn't important to buy some of these extras at first. You can add to your pantry gradually as you go shopping or when you need them.

It is good to have the ingredients on hand to make a few simple meals such as pasta dishes, soups, and grain and legume dinners such as rice and beans. Think about the kinds of foods you like to eat, and purchase the extra ingredients to have them on hand.

If you are on a tight budget, you can take care of these items as you go along. Plan your meals in advance and write out a shopping list. You can buy these extras at the beginning of the week and store them as you buy them.

An example of a vegan larder

Even though larders may differ from household to household, it will be helpful to view a sample pantry. You can use this as a starting point to help you to figure out how to stock yours, or you can take this list to the store and start shopping! It's up to you.

It may help to think of your larder in terms of categories such as breakfast items, snacks, etc. Here's a rough list:

Breakfast items
- Wholegrain hot cereals such as oatmeal or cream of wheat
- Cold cereals to eat with soya milk, nut milk, or rice milk
- Vegan-friendly pancake mixes
- Vegan baked goods such as muffins

Snacks
- A variety of healthy snack items such as granola bars
- Vegan treats such as cookies and cakes
- Crackers and other baked items

Miscellaneous items
- Nut milk, soya milk, rice milk, and tofu in special packaging to help store it in the pantry and stay fresh longer
- Soup mixes, dried and canned items and other boxed meal products such as vegan macaroni cheese
- Nuts and seeds such as almonds, sesame seeds, sunflower seeds, and pecans
- Pasta – look for wholewheat varieties
- Items like spaghetti sauce, capers, pickles, extra ketchup, salad dressings, etc.

Grains, beans & pulses

These are just a few examples. Buy things that are in accordance with your preferences.

- Rye
- Buckwheat
- Quinoa
- Wheat products
- Brown rice
- Oats
- Chickpeas (garbanzo beans)
- Kidney beans
- Black beans
- Cannellini beans
- Northern beans
- Black-eyed peas
- Split peas
- Gungo peas
- Butter beans
- Red lentils
- Green lentils
- Puy lentils

Condiments

- Coconut oil to cook with
- At least one kind of flavourful oil such as cold-pressed olive oil or roasted sesame oil
- Tamari and/or soy sauce
- Vinegar – you can keep several kinds on hand, such as balsamic, rice wine, and distilled vinegar
- Salt, pepper, herbs and spices

Baking items

- Leavening agents such as yeast, baking powder, and baking soda
- Vegan-friendly egg substitute
- Different kinds of flours: spelt, plain, self-raising, buckwheat, etc.
- Sugars and other sweetener products such as maple syrup, rice syrup and agave syrup

This list is designed to be just a starting point. It is almost impossible to come up with a blanket list because everyone's food preferences vary greatly. The approach most people like to take is to purchase things as and when they need them.

Remember to look at the ingredients, especially when you are buying packaged food. As we've explored, there are often hidden ingredients that are not vegan-friendly where you would least expect them.

Vegan Cooking Basics

So, we have spent some time thinking about some of the common ingredients that are usually included in vegan foods. We've learnt how to stock the pantry and also find hidden ingredients in foods that vegans should not eat. The next step is to actually learn how to cook.

If you already know how to cook, you can skip this section; but I would recommend reading it anyway, because there could be one or two things in here that you don't already know. To receive instruction in the best way, you really should cook with someone who knows what they are doing so that you can learn from them.

Or, better still, you can take some cooking classes. Search around your area to see if you can find any vegan cooking classes that can give you a good introduction to some of the techniques.

Even though we will go over the techniques you need to know to put together a variety of foods in this chapter, it can be fun learning in a group environment.

Here is a basic list of some of the techniques you need:
• Setting up your kitchen
• How to follow a recipe
• Basic cooking techniques

People could spend a lifetime learning how to cook and not even scratch the surface; so we'll go over some of the basic techniques. If you want to learn more, you should probably consider enrolling in a class.

Setting up your kitchen

As mentioned in the previous chapter, stocking your pantry is an important piece of the vegan cooking puzzle. The other is to have a well-equipped kitchen to cook a variety of recipes.

Now, there are two types of chefs out there: those who like to use a lot of gadgets, and those who don't. Most home cooks tend to fall somewhere in between.

Here's a list of some of the basic kitchen supplies you need to have on hand in order to be able to cook a variety of recipes. If you come across something that you want to make that calls for specialised equipment, you can either consider buying it or make a substitution.

- A good set of knives that includes a bread knife and a chef's knife. Unless they are serrated, make sure you keep them sharp. You'll also want a large cutting board.
- An electric mixer. If you do a lot of baking, you may want to find an upright mixer that sits on your countertop.
- Various utensils such as a pair of sturdy tongs, a sieve, wooden spoons, rubber spatulas, and a sturdy wire whisk.
- A small toaster oven and a microwave.
- A blender and/or a food processor.
- Optional, but nice to have on hand – a stick blender, a crockpot, an ice cream maker, and a bread maker if you love freshly baked bread.
- A good variety of pots, pans, baking dishes, and mixing bowls.

Some people make the mistake of buying everything at once. This is a mistake, especially if you're new to cooking. You'll start to understand your personal style.

How to follow recipes

Learning how to follow recipes is a very important skill to learning how to cook. Most recipes are pretty straightforward. However, it is easy to take them for granted until something is going wrong. There are many handwritten recipes out there that leave out crucial ingredients without meaning to. If you come across a recipe like this, having a good knowledge of how recipes work can help you identify the missing ingredient.

If you are just learning how to cook, you'll be following recipes all the time. However, as you get more comfortable in the kitchen, you'll gradually start to lose your dependence on them. After you follow a few recipes, you can start to write your own original dishes down. Just remember to list the ingredients in the order that they will appear in the instructions. This makes the recipe easier to follow.

Basic cooking techniques

After you set up your kitchen and you make sure you understand how to follow recipes, the next step is to learn some basic cooking techniques. Here is a short list of some of the things you'll need to do in order to cook.

How to use your knives

There is a right and a wrong way to chop. Most people don't think much about it. However, the wrong technique can get you injured and also make you inefficient. In order to learn, you'll want to work with a professional. Always make sure your knives are sharp, too. It's actually more dangerous if they're dull.

If you don't want to take cooking classes in order to learn proper chopping technique, you could always watch a cooking show on television and mimic what they do.

It is essential to have a high-quality chef's knife on hand. When cooking certain things, such as salads and soups, most of your time is spent chopping. If you learn how to be efficient you can save a lot of time.

The differences between boiling, heating, and simmering

These are three very basic cooking techniques for the stove top. Boiling is when you typically set the heat on high and wait for the mixture to bubble. Heating something is when you let it get hot but not boiling (so there won't be any bubbles). When you simmer something, you put it on low heat for a long amount of time. Things like soups and stews, for example, are typically simmered.

The difference between baking and grilling (USA: broiling)

The terms 'baking' and 'grilling' do not refer to the same thing. However, some things that can be baked can also be grilled, and vice versa. Baking happens at a lower heat than grilling. Classic things that are baked include breads, cookies, cakes, and savoury dishes such as vegetarian lasagna and roasted vegetables. Things like vegetarian lasagna, for example, can also be grilled.

Most ovens come equipped with a grill. However, each one is different. You'll need to read your manual in order to learn how to operate yours.

How to use all of your appliances

Another crucial step to creating vegan dishes is to make sure you understand how to use all of your appliances. For example, you may not realise it but your microwave may also have a fan-assisted oven setting. You may not realise what it's capable of until you read the manual.

Also, you'll be able to make adjustments in recipes according to how your appliances work. For example, if the instructions say to beat something on high for two minutes, your mixer could take longer if the 'high' setting is not as powerful as the mixer used to test and write the original recipe.

Common cooking terms and what they mean

Once you get acquainted with your kitchen and start following some recipes, you may come across some terms that you don't know what to do with. Here are some common ones you may encounter:

Mashing

You can either mash with your fork, if it is a smaller portion, or with a masher tool. Some people prefer to whip things that are normally mashed, such as potatoes or squash.

Whip

You can use a hand mixer, an upright mixer, or a wire whisk to whip just about anything.

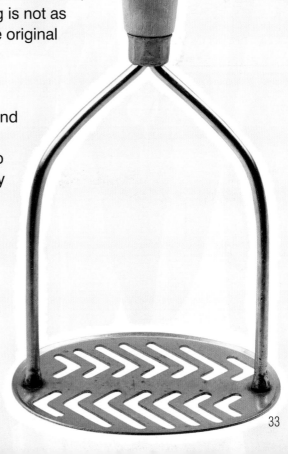

Crush

You can crush things with the back of your knife, the bottom of a glass, or other heavy objects. There are also special kitchen gadgets used for crushing.

Grate

Graters come in different forms. Just take your pick. If you need to grate an orange peel or lemon peel, a small, handheld grater is best.

Knife techniques

There are several different kinds of knife techniques you can use, including chop, julienne (into matchstick-sized pieces), crush, and slice.

Blend

Depending on what you are blending you have three choices – a regular blender, a handheld stick blender (which works best for soups), and a food processor. The tool you use will depend on the recipe.

Purée

When a recipe tells you to purée something, you can do it in small batches in the regular blender, use a stick blender, or use the food processor.

This is just an overview of some of the techniques you will encounter. A good, comprehensive cookbook will help you define any other terms you need to learn – or you can look online.

Conversions

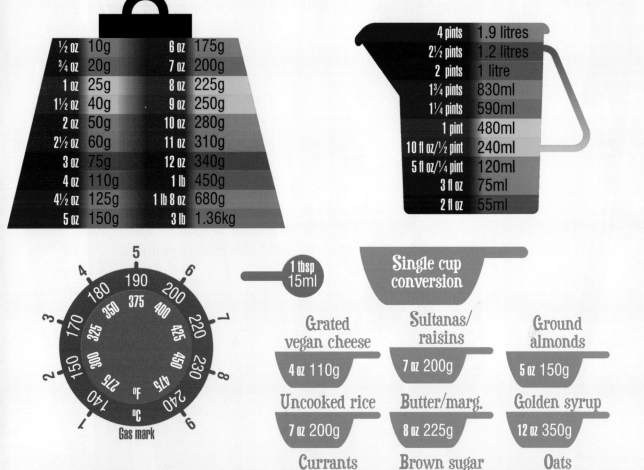

½ oz	10g	6 oz	175g
¾ oz	20g	7 oz	200g
1 oz	25g	8 oz	225g
1½ oz	40g	9 oz	250g
2 oz	50g	10 oz	280g
2½ oz	60g	11 oz	310g
3 oz	75g	12 oz	340g
4 oz	110g	1 lb	450g
4½ oz	125g	1 lb 8 oz	680g
5 oz	150g	3 lb	1.36kg

4 pints	1.9 litres
2½ pints	1.2 litres
2 pints	1 litre
1¾ pints	830ml
1¼ pints	590ml
1 pint	480ml
10 fl oz/½ pint	240ml
5 fl oz/¼ pint	120ml
3 fl oz	75ml
2 fl oz	55ml

Gas mark

°F / °C

1 tbsp 15ml

Single cup conversion

Grated vegan cheese	Sultanas/ raisins	Ground almonds
4 oz 110g	7 oz 200g	5 oz 150g
Uncooked rice	**Butter/marg.**	**Golden syrup**
7 oz 200g	8 oz 225g	12 oz 350g
Currants	**Brown sugar**	**Oats**
5 oz 150g	6 oz 175g	4 oz 110g
Flour	**White sugar**	**1 stick butter**
5 oz 150g	8 oz 225g	4 oz 110g

Liquid

1 cup	½ pint	250ml
½ cup	¼ pint	125ml
¼ cup	4 tbsp	60ml

A standard metric cup holds 250ml (an American cup holds slightly less, but as long as you stick to one measure or the other your recipes will convert).

When measuring dry ingredients, it is advisable to level off the cup with the back of a knife, without tapping or shaking the cup (as this packs down the ingredients and doesn't give a true measure). A set of measuring cups and spoons can be bought from most supermarkets and department stores, and they are usually quite cheaply priced.

Kitchen Tools

Having a good selection of kitchen tools will make your cooking experience much more efficient and even more fun.

Measuring spoon

A measuring spoon is a spoon used to measure an amount of an ingredient, either liquid or dry, when cooking. Measuring spoons may be made of plastic, metal, or other materials. They are available in many sizes, including the teaspoon (tsp) and tablespoon (tbsp).

Blender

A blender is your best friend in the kitchen and can be used for so many things, such as sauces, purées, smoothies and so on. Using a blender can make your cooking experience so much easier. Even if you have a simple, low-budget blender it still helps to ease the workload in the kitchen, so it's a great investment.

Colander

A colander is a cheap piece of equipment that makes washing fruits and vegetables much easier and can also save on wasting water.

Cutting boards

Cutting boards can be made of wood or plastic; my preference is plastic, as they tend to be easier to sanitise.

Electric hand mixer

Hand mixers are really helpful for making cakes, puddings and batters, and even kneading dough.

Food processor

This will save you a lot of hard work when you have to slice, dice, grate or shred.

Measuring cups

Measuring cups come in a variety of sizes and are used to measure the volume of liquid or solid cooking ingredients such as flour and sugar, especially for volumes from about 50ml (2 fl oz) upwards.

Spatula

A spatula is a must-have kitchen utensil used for mixing and spreading things.

Strainer/sieve

This is a device that has holes punched in it or is made of crossed wires for separating solid matter from a liquid. This can also be used for sifting flour.

Vegetable peeler

Save time, effort and energy by having a vegetable peeler. It usually consists of a slotted metal blade attached to a handle that is used to remove the outer skin or peel of certain vegetables, often potatoes and carrots, and fruits such as apples and pears.

Recipes

BREAKFAST

Breakfast is eaten by everyone everywhere in the world. However, the type of food eaten varies from one country to another. Children are usually quite active and are in need of good nutrition in order for health and growth. Give your little ones a good meal to get them started. Even fussy eaters can be encouraged by involving them in the process of preparing breakfast and helping to choose what is on the menu for breakfast.

Breakfast is a meal that can sometimes be underestimated. Having a good breakfast to start is always a good thing to do. Try being a bit creative and add some variety to the first meal of the day. I love to have a back-up breakfast just in case I wake up late one morning. I try and prepare my breakfasts at the beginning of the week so that when my hectic schedule begins I know exactly what I will be having, and that takes the stress out of trying to find something healthy and nutritious when you're in a hurry.

25 mins

4 portions

Baked Banana, Cinnamon & Raisin Pancakes

These pancakes are so quick and easy to make. They can also be made the night before and gently heated when you are ready to eat them. Try out different toppings and add the fruit or sauce of your choice. My favourite toppings are blueberries and maple syrup or chopped mango, pineapple and banana.

1 Preheat oven to 180°C (350°F or gas mark 4).

2 Line a large baking tray with baking paper or grease-proof paper.

3 Combine the **oat flour, wholemeal flour, baking powder, cinnamon** and **salt**.

4 Stir well.

5 Add **banana** to the **dry ingredients**.

6 Add the **almond milk** and raisins.

7 Stir well.

8 Place ¼ of the mixture onto the baking tray to form 4 pancakes.

9 Bake for about 12-15 minutes.

10 Allow to cool slightly and serve topped with fruit or a sauce of your choice.

Shopping list

Oats – 1 cup (finely ground into a flour-type mixture by blending for about 30 seconds)
Spelt **or** wholegrain flour – ¼ cup
Baking powder – 1½ tsp
Cinnamon – ½ tsp
Salt – ¼ tsp
Banana – 1 large ripe, finely mashed
Almond milk – 1¼ cups
Raisins – ¼ cup

Plantain Porridge

BREAKFAST

40 mins

4 portions

Plantains make a wonderful porridge. Sometimes, when plain old oats are not interesting enough, you can add some interest by making this — and it's so simple to make, too. Plantains are available across the globe. In Europe we can get them in most African, Caribbean or Asian grocer shops.

1 Wash and peel the skin from the plantains.

2 Grate the plantains.

3 Add flour and salt and mix well.

4 Beat mixture with a fork and enough water to make a smooth batter.

5 Bring water to boil, add coconut milk, and simmer on low heat to avoid liquid boiling over.

6 Pour liquid into plantain mixture, a bit at a time. Stir constantly to avoid lumps until mixture thickens.

7 Let simmer over low heat for 20 to 30 minutes.

8 Sweeten with sugar, honey or molasses to taste.

9 Sprinkle cinnamon, vanilla or grated nutmeg on top.

 ## Shopping list

Plantains – 3 ripe, peeled and grated
Coconut milk – 1 cup
Flour – ½ cup
Pinch of salt
Sugar (preferably brown) or molasses, to taste
Nutmeg – ¼ tsp
Vanilla – ½ tsp
Cinnamon – ¼ tsp

Aunty Verna's Granola

40 mins

6-8 portions

This recipe is named after my Aunty Verna, as she taught me to make this lovely and versatile breakfast. Serve with non-dairy milk or use as a topping on non-dairy ice cream. I also use it as a snack. I store portions in small plastic containers and eat from them with a spoon when I'm out and about.

1 Preheat oven to 180°C (350°F; gas mark 4).

2 Mix together the oats, sugar and coconut.

3 In a separate container add nutmeg, cinnamon, pinch of salt, almond essence and rose water to the orange juice.

4 Add the orange juice mixture to the oats mixture.

5 Stir with clean hands until all of mixture is moist.

6 Place on baking sheets and spread out into one even layer.

7 Stir every 10-15 minutes.

8 During the final 10 minutes add the nuts and seeds.

9 Allow to cool, then store in airtight containers.

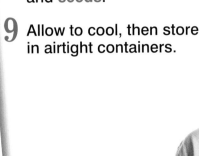

Shopping list

Rolled oats – 500-700g
    (old-fashioned large-grained type)
Coconut – ¼ cup (half shredded
    and half grated)
Unrefined brown sugar – 3 tbsp
Oranges – juice of 3 large
Nutmeg – ½ tsp
Cinnamon – ½ tsp
Pinch of salt
Almond essence – 1 tsp
Rose water – 1 tsp
Peanuts – ½ cup crushed
Sunflower seeds – ½ cup
Sesame seeds – ½ cup
Flax seeds (linseed) – ¼ cup

46

Berry Breakfast Smoothie

BREAKFAST

10 mins

2 portions

Smoothies are a great way to start your day and consume lots of fruits and vegetables in one serving. It's also a great way to use up the fruits in your fruit bowl. If you have a low appetite, it is a good way to get some nutrients when you don't feel much like eating.

1 Mix **all ingredients** together in blender.

2 Blend until smooth.

3 Pour into 2 chilled glasses.

Shopping list

Raspberries – 1 cup (7 oz; 200g) frozen or fresh, unsweetened

Almond or rice milk – ¾ cup (6 fl oz; 177ml) chilled, unsweetened

Cherries/raspberries – ¼ cup (2 oz; 50g) frozen or fresh, pitted

Dates – 4, pitted and chopped

Ginger – 2 tsp finely grated, fresh

Flaxseed (linseed) – 1 tsp ground

Lemon juice – 1 tsp fresh

Sunshine Smoothie

BREAKFAST

10 mins

2 portions

Create your own sunshine in a cup with this great smoothie recipe that is both delicious and nutritious. It is packed with tropical fruits that are always a popular favourite. You can prepare the fruits the night before, and then blend them just before you are ready to serve.

1 Mix **all ingredients** together in blender.

2 Blend until smooth.

Shopping list

Pineapple – 1-2 cups (peeled and chopped)
Mango – 1 (peeled, deseeded and chopped)
Bananas – 2 ripe (peeled and chopped)
Rice milk/unsweetened coconut milk
   or water – 1 cup
Flaxseed (linseed) – 1 teaspoon ground,
   golden

Vanilla Overnight Oats

This is a great time-saver, as you make it the night before and all you need to do the next day is to enjoy. It's also a great one to make if you are going on a car journey, as you can take it with you and eat it on the way. It does not require any heating and is a good way to start the day.

1 Mix **all ingredients** together in a mixing bowl.

2 Spoon into a jar with a tight-fitting lid.

3 Close and refrigerate for at least four hours, but preferably overnight, before eating.

Shopping list

Plain non-dairy yoghurt – ⅓ cup
Rolled oats – ½ cup (heaped)
Unsweetened almond milk – ⅔ cup
Flax meal (linseed meal) – 1 tbsp ground
Vanilla extract – ½ tsp
Pinch of salt
Agave or maple syrup – 2 tbsp

55 mins

8-12 portions

Light and Fluffy Cornmeal Muffins

Cornmeal muffins are quick and easy to make and can be made just before you need to serve them. They taste great with peanut butter and jam. In addition, they also taste great with baked beans or chilli. They work well as finger food at a party, too.

1 Preheat your oven to 180°C (350°F).

2 Grease the muffin tin or loaf tin (this recipe can make one loaf or a dozen muffins).

3 In a large bowl, measure out **all of the dry ingredients** (flours, baking powder, salt), and in a smaller bowl measure out **all of the wet ingredients**.

4 Pour the **wet ingredients** into the **dry ingredients** and stir them together till just combined. Now pour the whole mixture into your oiled muffin tin or loaf tin.

5 Bake for 30-45 minutes, or until a toothpick inserted into the middle comes out clean.

6 Allow to cool.

Shopping list

Cornmeal – 2 cups coarse
Wholewheat flour – 1½ cups
Unbleached plain flour – ½ cup
Baking powder – 1 tbsp + 1 tsp
Salt – 2 tsp
Maple syrup, honey, or agave syrup – ⅔ cup
Soya or coconut milk – 2 cups at room temperature
Oil (olive, canola, or rapeseed) – ½ cup

5 mins

1-2 portions

Blueberry Overnight Oats

Blueberries are a super food, so they are a good ingredient for a breakfast dish. If you don't have any blueberries you can use whichever berries you have available — like raspberries, blackberries or strawberries. You can also use cherries. For a gluten-free option, use gluten-free oats.

1 Mix **all ingredients** together in a medium-sized mixing bowl, reserving a few blueberries and almonds.

2 Spoon into a jar with a tight-fitting lid.

3 Close and refrigerate for at least 4 hours, but preferably overnight, before eating.

4 Garnish with the reserved **blueberries** and **almonds** to serve.

Shopping list

Banana – 1, mashed
Old-fashioned dry oats – ⅓ cup
Non-dairy, fat-free yoghurt – 1 tub
Blueberries – ⅓ cup
Almonds – ⅓ cup, chopped

Crazy Pink Smoothie Bowl

5 mins

1-2 portions

A 'smoothie bowl' smoothie is thicker in consistency than a regular smoothie. Popular 'smoothie bowl' toppings include pumpkin seeds, sunflower seeds, granola or muesli to add a bit of crunch. The smoothie bowl is the base and toppings usually include fruits, nuts, seeds and sometimes edible flowers.

1 Combine **all ingredients** in blender.

2 Blend until smooth.

3 Decorate with chopped fruits, nuts or seeds and serve.

Shopping list

Beetroot – ¼ medium-sized, peeled
Apples – 2 medium, cored and chopped
Bananas – 2, peeled and chopped
Chia seeds – 1 tsp ground
Dates – 3, pitted
Peanut butter – 1 tsp

Jungle Green Smoothie Bowl

BREAKFAST

5 mins

1-2 portions

If Tarzan were choosing a smoothie bowl I think this would be his favourite: packed with great green stuff, just the way he would like it. Smoothie bowls are a great way to encourage little ones to eat more fruit and vegetables without them even realising it!

1 Combine **all ingredients** in blender.

2 Blend until smooth.

3 Decorate with chopped fruits, nuts or seeds and serve.

Shopping list

Kale **or** spinach – ½ **cup** chopped
Apples – **2 medium,** cored and chopped
Banana – **1,** peeled and chopped
Flaxseed (golden linseed) – **1 tsp** ground

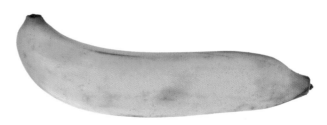

LUNCHBOX

Trying to figure out what to put in a lunchbox can sometimes be quite frustrating. Many people have asked me over and over again what goes into a vegan lunchbox. There are many more options than you think, and the trick is to keep a list of ideas and add to it when you discover new ideas.

Lunchbox items can be so versatile, from a flask of soup in the colder months to fresh fruit and vegetable sticks in the warmer months of the year. Sandwiches are great, but you can also vary the bread and also try pitta bread, wraps, flatbread – the choices are endless. The key is to be creative and share ideas with others, and don't be afraid to try new ideas. Oh, and don't forget that leftovers from dinner can make great lunches too!

10 mins

1-2 portions

Salad in a Jar – Traffic Light

Salad is a great option for lunch, and you can use either a glass jar or a plastic jar that is BPA-free. To serve the salad just tip it out into a plate or bowl, or you can even just eat it straight from the jar if it's not packed too tightly

Layer the salad in the jar in this order:

1 **Vegan mayonnaise** (place this in first so that the whole salad doesn't go soggy)

2 **Cherry tomatoes** (heavier ingredients are best placed in second so that they don't weigh down the salad)

3 **Sweetcorn**

4 **Lettuce or spinach leaves**

5 **Pumpkin seeds**

6 **Sunflower seeds**

Cover the jar and store in the fridge until ready to serve

Shopping list

Vegan mayonnaise – 2-3 tbsp
Cherry tomatoes – 5-7
Sweetcorn – 3-4 tbsp
Lettuce or spinach – 8-10 leaves
Pumpkin seeds – 2-3 tsp
Sunflower seeds – 2-3 tsp

10 mins

1-2 portions

Salad in a Jar – Chick-green-pep-spin

Salads that you make yourself work out much cheaper than buying lunch. The varieties of salads you can make are endless. There are so many flavours and ingredients you can make with this: you name it, you can make a salad in a jar with it.

Salad dressing:

1 Combine all ingredients, mix well and serve.

Layer the salad in the jar in this order:

1 **Salad dressing** (place this in first so that the whole salad doesn't go soggy)

2 **Chickpeas** (place in second so that they don't weigh down the salad)

3 Cooked green peas

4 Bell pepper

5 Lettuce or spinach leaves

6 Sesame seeds

Cover the jar and store in the fridge until ready to serve.

Shopping list

Vegan mayonnaise – 2-3 tbsp
Chickpeas – 4-5 tbsp
Green peas – 3-4 tbsp, cooked
Bell pepper – ¼, red, chopped
Lettuce or spinach – 4-5 leaves
Sesame seeds – 2 tsp

For the dressing:
Extra virgin olive oil – 3 tbsp
Fresh lemon juice – 1-2 tbsp
Salt – pinch
Freshly ground black pepper – ¼ tsp

Fruit Salad in a Jar

10 mins

1-2 portions

Now you can eat a rainbow for dessert. This is a great way to use up lots of fruits and also to encourage your child to eat more fruit. You can get them to make this with you as they will have fun filling the jar with some of their favourite fruits.

Layer the salad in the jar in this order:

1 Kiwi

2 Plums

3 Orange

4 Blueberries

5 Pink grapefruit

6 Mango

7 Raspberries

Cover the jar and store in the fridge until ready to serve.

Shopping list

Kiwi – 1, chopped
Plums – 2, peeled and chopped
Orange – ½, peeled and chopped
Blueberries – 2-3 tbsp
Pink grapefruit – ¼, peeled and chopped
Mango – ½, peeled and chopped
Raspberries – 2-3 tbsp

Sandwiches

Sometimes we can get stuck for ideas on what to put in our sandwiches. The simple sandwich can be boring, but at the same time it can be exciting if you have some ideas on how to make it a little more interesting. Variety is definitely the spice of life, so try out some new ideas when it comes to making the humble sandwich. To vary your sandwich making, try to use different kinds of bread. There are so many different ones available these days, including:

- Hard dough bread
- Wholemeal hard dough bread
- Wholemeal bread
- Sourdough bread
- Pitta bread
- Spelt bread
- Rye bread
- Challah bread

Be creative with the fillings – there are so many different ones to choose from these days! I'm giving you a few of my favourites to get you started.

Sandwich and vegetable cutters are a great
way to add extra interest to your child's lunchbox!

Tasty Traffic Light:
Avocado, cherry tomatoes,
sweet yellow pepper
and lettuce

Strawberry Almond Dream:
Almond butter and
strawberry jam

Monkey's Favourite:
Banana and chopped dates

71

Bunny's Favourite:
Hummus and carrot

Bean Salad Feast:
Seasoned black beans,
sweet yellow pepper,
tomato and avocado

Red Beet:
Beetroot, lettuce,
red onion and
sweet mustard sauce

Great Green Stuff:
Sliced avocado and lettuce
with dash of olive oil and a
sprinkle of salt

The Sweet Egyptian:
Chopped falafel,
spinach and
sweet chilli sauce

Funky Monkey Treat:
Peanut butter, banana
and a dash of maple syrup

73

Flour

There is a growing number of different types of flour that are readily available in most major supermarkets across the world. They are not all the same, and using the wrong flour in your baking recipe can result in a baking disaster!

Some of my favourites are the healthier choices, which include:

- Spelt flour – bread, puddings, cakes, cookies
- Buckwheat flour – pancakes, pasta, crêpes
- Wholewheat flour – pastry, bread, cakes, cookies, puddings
- Unbleached flour – bread, cakes, cookies, biscuits, pancakes
- Coconut flour – cakes, puddings, pancakes

Different flours explained

Spelt

Spelt is a type of wheat. Its nutrition content is very similar to other types of wheat, and it is high in gluten.

Buckwheat

Buckwheat flour is ground from buckwheat. Although treated as a grain, buckwheat is not a cereal or grass, but it is actually a fruit that is closely related to wild rhubarb.

Wholewheat

Wholewheat flour has more fibre than white flour, and is therefore more nutritious.

Unbleached

A lot of white flour is bleached, but you can get unbleached white flour. Bleached flour is treated with chemical agents to speed up ageing, while unbleached flour is bleached naturally as it ages.

Coconut

Coconut flour is a gluten-free 'flour' that is basically dried coconut in a powdered form.

LUNCHBOX

45 mins

4 portions

Quick and Easy Fruit Bread

Everyone likes homemade bread, but it can seem a really daunting task if you have to make it yourself — so here is a really quick and tasty bread that is super easy to make and doesn't need to be left to rise. You can make this with or without the fruit, whichever is your preference.

1 Mix together the flour, salt, sugar, oil and mixed fruit.

2 Make a well in the middle of the mixture and then pour in the water.

3 Stir.

4 Turn out onto a floured surface and lightly shape into a flat circle.

5 Make indentations using a wooden spoon so that it looks like a clock face.

6 Bake at 200°C (400°F; gas mark 6) for about 30 minutes.

Shopping list

Self-raising flour – 450g
Salt – ½ tsp
Extra virgin olive oil – 1 tbsp, light
Dried fruit – 200g, mixed
Sugar – 50g, brown
Warm water – 225ml

LUNCHBOX

60 mins

1 portions

Coconut, Cinnamon & Raisin Spelt Bread

I made this recipe using spelt flour and hesitated at first, as I thought it would come out dry and dense, but surprisingly it came out quite light and is not dry either, with a great flavour. I don't usually use spelt flour, but I am pleased with this recipe as I became more adventurous with ingredients!

1 Preheat oven to 180°C (350°F; gas mark 4).

2 Mix together flour, baking powder, baking soda, cinnamon.

3 Add agave syrup, coconut milk, banana, raisins.

4 Stir just enough to combine ingredients.

5 Put mixture into a medium-sized greased loaf tin and bake for 40-45 minutes.

6 Test with a toothpick or cake tester: if it comes out clean the loaf is ready.

7 Remove from tin and cool on a wire rack.

Shopping list

Wholewheat spelt flour – 2 cups
Baking powder – 1 tsp
Bicarbonate of soda (baking soda) – 1 tsp
Cinnamon – ¼ tsp
Agave syrup or maple syrup – ¼ cup
Banana – 1 small, mashed
Raisins – 1 cup
Coconut milk – 1 cup, thick

This can be eaten on its own or spread with vegan butter.

Midweek meals can be a delight or a chore. Planning ahead is the key to making them more of a delight! Dinner is the meal that brings the family back together after a day at work or school. I try to plan my dinner menu at the beginning of the week. However, I am not always able to do that, so I sometimes plan for the next two or three days. I also use my store cupboard and fridge when planning so that I use up the ingredients that I already have, so as not to waste food.

I am sometimes not sure what to include on the menu when planning dinners in advance, so I will use my extensive range of cookbooks and also watch cooking programmes to get ideas. Another good idea is to swap meal plans with a friend.

40 mins

6-8 portions

Sweet Potato Burgers

I love sweet potato, and I just created this recipe that makes it into a great burger. I also added a little Jamaican seasoning to put a little sunshine in the recipe! This can be served in a burger bun with fries. It can also be served with salad in a wrap/roti.

1 Combine all ingredients together and mix well.

2 Use 2 tbsp of the mixture to form each burger (use a medium cookie cutter to help you).

3 Place burgers on greased baking tray.

4 Bake for 25-30 minutes at 180°C (350°F; gas mark 4).

5 Turn burgers over halfway through cooking time.

6 Allow to cool and then serve.

Shopping list

Sweet potato – 1 medium (approx. 1 cup), boiled and mashed
Wheatgerm – 1½ cups
Instant oats – 1 cup
Salt – ¼ tsp
Mixed herbs – ½ tsp
All-purpose seasoning (season-all) – 1-2 tsp
Garlic – 1 clove (minced)
Onion – 1 small, finely chopped
Almond milk – 1 cup
Bragg Aminos or soy sauce – 2 tbsp

45 mins

4 portions

Chunky Vegetable Soup

Vegetable soup is quick and easy to make and is a great way to get little ones to enjoy different vegetables. I vary the vegetables I use as it keeps the soup interesting and is also a great way to use up any vegetables you have in your kitchen. Your child can help you to make this soup by choosing which vegetables they would like to put into the soup and also choosing what type of bread rolls to serve with the soup.

1 In a large saucepan, add the olive oil and fry the onion, garlic, carrot, celery and thyme for 3-4 minutes over a medium heat until they begin to soften.

2 Add the sweet potato, tomatoes, coconut milk, vegetable stock and bay leaves.

3 Bring to a steady simmer and cook for 20 minutes, stirring occasionally.

4 Add the chickpeas and continue cooking for a further 10-15 minutes, and then serve.

Shopping list

Olive oil – 2 tbsp
Onions – 2, roughly chopped
Garlic – 1 clove, chopped
Carrot – 1, peeled and finely chopped
Celery – 3 sticks, finely chopped
Thyme – 2 sprigs
Sweet potatoes – 2 small, peeled and cubed
Tomatoes – 1 cup/250g/9 oz, chopped
Coconut milk – 1 cup/250ml/9fl oz
Vegetable stock – 2 cups/500ml/¾ pint
Bay leaves – 3
Chickpeas – 1½ cups/250g/9 oz, cooked

Butter Bean Falafels

Butter beans have a subtle flavour, so they are great for young ones to try as a new dish. Can be used as a main course (serve with rice and gravy) or side dish (serve with a sauce).

1 Finely dice the onion.

2 In a bowl, mash butter beans with a fork or potato masher.

3 Mix into the beans the onion, garlic, chillies, turmeric, salt, pepper and herbs.

4 Thoroughly mix up ingredients using your hands or a food processor. (Using a food processor will create a smoother texture.)

5 Mix in flour until mix becomes drier.

6 Put some flour on surface and on hands and shape falafel mix into small balls, roll in flour and press down gently to form thick discs.

7 Bake in a medium oven for 20 to 30 minutes or until golden brown.

 Shopping list

Butter beans – 1 can (drained)
Onion – 1 medium
Garlic – 1 tbsp
Garam masala – ½ tsp
Turmeric – 1 tbsp
Flour – 2 tbsp
Herbs – 2 tsp mixed, dried
Salt – ½ tsp
Black pepper – 1 tsp

Falafels are great served warm or cold with hummus or pitta bread, or in a wrap. The patties could also be made bigger to form a substitute for a bean burger.

Stew Peas with Spinners

This is my vegan version of a Jamaican classic. Spinners are a type of dumpling made from flour and water, often added to soups and stews in Jamaican cuisine.

80 mins

4 portions

Stew

1 Put the soaked kidney beans and garlic together in a pan and boil until the beans are tender (about an hour and a half).

2 Add the coconut milk, spring onions, scotch bonnet pepper (very hot red chilli peppers – if using), thyme and seasonings and simmer for 40 minutes.

Spinners

1 Put the flour and salt in a medium bowl.

2 Add enough water to bind, then work the mixture with your hands to make a stiff dough.

3 Roll it into slim, inch-long pieces.

4 Drop the spinners into the stew, cover and cook for around 20 minutes.

5 Mix the three tablespoons of flour with the four tablespoons of water, then add to the stew and stir.

6 Boil until the stew thickens, stirring occasionally to prevent sticking.

7 Serve with plain rice.

Shopping list

Kidney beans – 2 cups (370g; 13 oz), soaked overnight
Garlic – 3 cloves
Coconut milk – 2 cups (500ml; 1 pint)
Spring onions (scallions) – 2, chopped
Thyme – 3 sprigs
Pimento seeds – 6, crushed
Season-all – 2 level tsp
Salt and pepper – to taste
Flour – 3 tbsp
Water – 4 tbsp

For the spinners:
Flour – 1 cup (150g; 5 oz)
Salt – ½ tsp
Water to bind

80 mins

4-6 portions

Butternut Squash & Sweet Potato Soup

Soups are great any time of year, and this quick and easy soup is delicious and can be made in advance of when you need it. I like to make this when I am busy, and it goes down well when I am cooking for children.

1 Make some small slashes in the butternut squash so that it bakes evenly.

2 Bake the butternut squash in a medium oven (180°C; 350°F) for about 45 mins or until soft.

3 Cut open the butternut squash and scoop out the seeds.

4 Peel and chop the butternut squash and then place it in a medium-sized pot.

5 Add 4 cups of water and a vegetable stock cube.

6 Next add plantain, baked sweet potato, garlic, mixed herbs, pepper, salt and all-purpose seasoning.

7 Cook on a low-to-medium heat for about 30 minutes.

Shopping list

Butternut squash – 1 small to medium, baked, then peeled and deseeded
Water – 4 cups
Vegetable stock cube – 1
Plantain – 1, peeled and chopped
Garlic – 2 cloves, finely minced
All-purpose seasoning – 1-2 tbsp
Sweet potatoes – 1-2 small, baked and peeled
Mixed herbs – to taste
Salt and pepper – to taste

If you prefer a smooth soup, cool and blend until you get to the consistency you want. Serve with seeds or a dash of balsamic vinegar for extra tang.

Sweet Chicks

If your child likes sweet things then this will be a great delight for both you and your child. The sweet taste comes from the sweet potato and it is made using only healthy ingredients so it's a win-win situation if you are trying to get your child to control their sugar intake.

1 Chop 10-15 sweet potatoes in half, and place on a baking sheet.

2 Sprinkle with salt, and spray with cooking oil.

3 Bake at 200°C (400°F; gas mark 6) for 40 minutes, or until soft.

4 Scoop out a small section of the sweet potatoes to create a bowl. (You can add these to the filling mixture.)

5 In a food processor, combine all remaining ingredients and blend thoroughly.

6 Add more water as needed, until the mixture is smooth and creamy.

7 Spoon mixture into a piping bag, and fill the potato cups.

8 Use a ridged tip on the bag for a beautiful textured effect!

9 Sprinkle with paprika and chives.

Shopping list

Sweet potatoes – Several small
Chickpeas – 15 oz (cooked)
Lemon juice – 1 tbsp
Garlic powder – 1 tbsp
Dijon mustard – 1 tsp
Turmeric – 1 tsp
Tahini – 2 tbsp
Water – 2 tbsp (add more as needed for a creamier texture)
Salt – to taste
Pepper – to taste

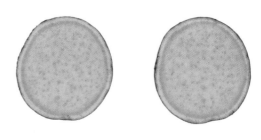

92

Meatless Loaf

45 mins

4-6 portions

Loaves are so versatile, because you can serve them for dinner with some nice roasted vegetables or you can slice them to put in a wrap or bread roll with salad. I like to make a loaf at the beginning of the week and then use it to make a few other meals. This is a great way to get children to eat more beans and pulses (if they are not already great fans of beans and pulses)!

1 Preheat the oven to 175°C (375°F; gas mark 4).

2 In a food processor, pulse the oats until well chopped but not pulverised.

3 Add the onion, green pepper, garlic and sunflower seeds and pulse again until well combined.

4 Add in the chickpeas, pinto beans, chilli powder, vegan Worcestershire sauce, salt and pepper.

5 Pulse until the chickpeas and beans are nearly puréed, but leave a bit of texture.

6 Spoon the bean mixture into a greased loaf pan and even out.

7 In a small bowl, whisk together all the glaze ingredients and then spread over the top of the loaf.

8 Bake for 30 to 35 minutes or until the glaze is caramelised and the loaf is firm.

9 Serve with the gravy found on the next page and a selection of vegetables.

Shopping list

Oats – 1 cup/100g/3½ oz
Onion – 1 small, diced
Green bell pepper – ½ large, diced
Garlic – 2 cloves
Sunflower seeds – ½ cup/75g/2½ oz
Chickpeas – 1½ cups/250g/9 oz, tinned or cooked
Pinto beans – 1½ cups/250g/9 oz, tinned or cooked
Chilli powder – ¼ tsp
Vegan Worcestershire sauce – 2 tbsp
Salt and pepper – to taste

For the glaze:
Tomato ketchup – ½ cup/110g/4 oz
Molasses – 2 tbsp
Chilli powder – 1 tsp
Vegan Dijon mustard – 2 tbsp
Water – ¼ cup/60ml/4 tbsp

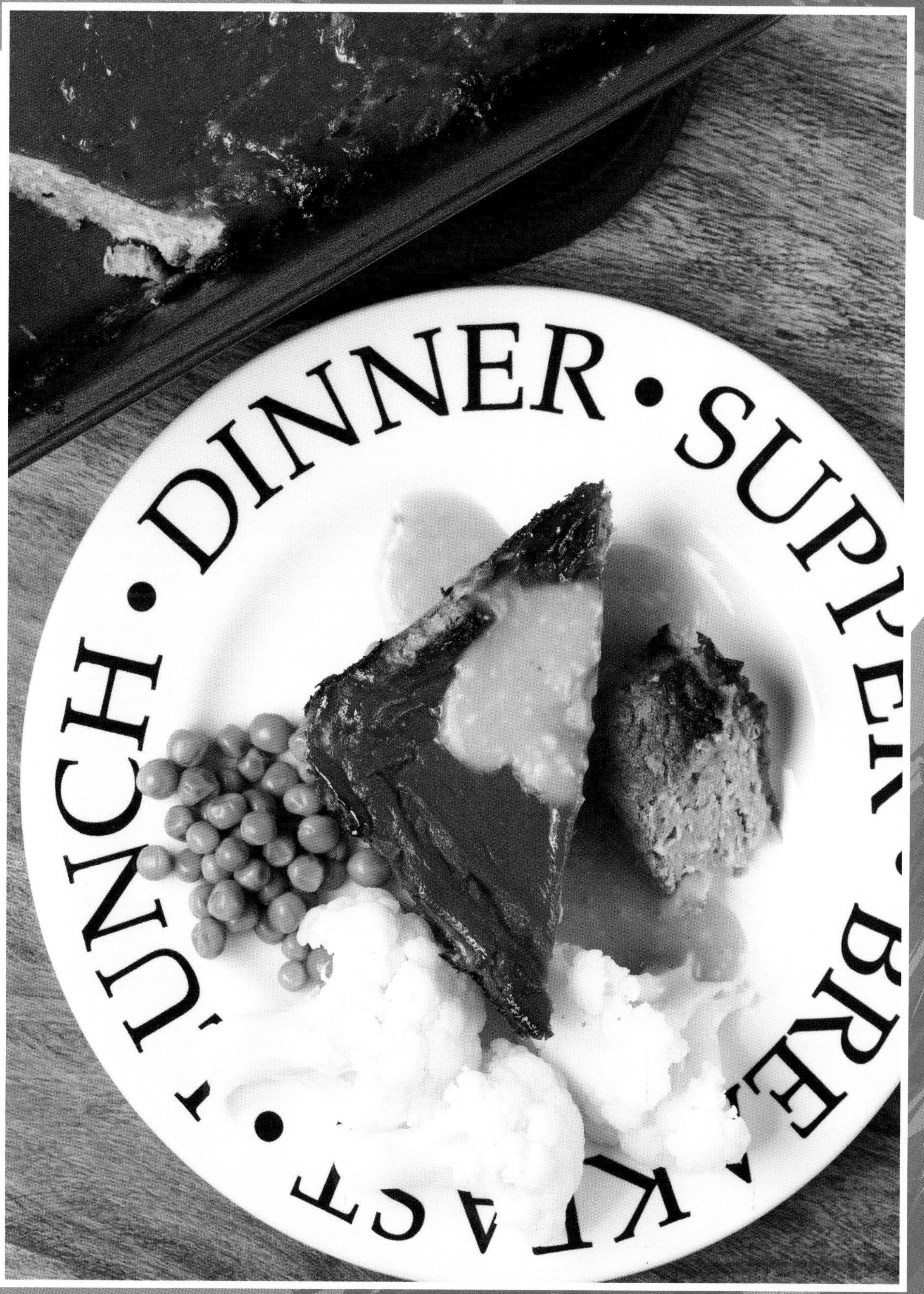
DINNER
SUPPER

Gravy

This gravy recipe is great with my meatless loaf from the previous page.

1 Fry the onion in the olive oil at a medium-high heat until it starts to brown.

2 Add the flour and mix until it starts to brown and stick to the onion.

3 Slowly stir in the bouillon, little by little.

4 Increase the heat and stir until the gravy reaches the boil. (Don't worry about any lumps. These can be strained out at the end. If the gravy is too thin, add some more flour and stir well.)

5 Add the soy sauce and seasonings. (Taste it before adding the salt – you may find it's already salty enough for your taste.)

6 Serve with the meatless loaf and a selection of vegetables.

DINNER

40 mins

2 portions

Shopping list

Onion – 1 medium, diced
Olive oil for sautéing
Flour – 3 tbsp
Vegan bouillon – 2 cups (500ml; ¾ pint)
Soy sauce – 1 tbsp
Cayenne pepper – pinch of (optional)
Salt and black pepper – to taste

Vegetable & Potato Bake

Need a quick and easy and healthy recipe that uses up vegetables or hides them from your little ones? Then look no further. Tray bakes are great if you have a few guests and you can get your children to choose the vegetables they would like to include.

1 Preheat the oven to 180°C (350°F; gas mark 4).

2 Heat the olive oil in a pan and then soften the onion for around five minutes, or until translucent.

3 Add the sliced pepper and cook for a further five minutes.

4 In a baking tray, layer the onion and pepper with the potato, tomato and chives, seasoning as you go.

5 Warm the rice milk with the stock cube and pour over the potatoes until barely covered.

6 Drizzle with a little more olive oil, cover, then bake for about an hour until the potatoes are tender, removing the cover after the first half-hour.

Shopping list

Olive oil – 1 tbsp
Onion – 1, peeled and sliced
Red bell pepper – 1 large, deseeded and sliced
Potatoes – 400g (14 oz), peeled and sliced
Tomatoes – 2 beef, sliced
Chives – 1 tbsp, chopped
Rice milk – 2½ cups (600ml; 1 pint)
Vegetable stock – 1 cube
Sea salt and freshly ground black pepper

DINNER

40 mins

4-6 portions

Red Lentil & Coconut Soup

I've been making this tasty recipe for years. I love red lentils as they are so easy to cook and in most countries they are a really cheap ingredient. The coconut gives it a rich (but not too rich) flavour. Serve this with some homemade bread rolls.

1 Heat the **oil** in a large saucepan over a medium heat and cook the **onions**, **ginger**, **garlic** and **fenugreek** (if using) until the onion is tender.

2 Add the **lentils**, **squash** and **coriander** into the pot.

3 Stir in the **water**, **coconut milk** and **tomato purée**.

4 Season with **curry powder**, **cayenne pepper**, **nutmeg**, **salt** and **pepper**.

5 Bring to a boil, then reduce the heat and simmer for 30 minutes, or until the lentils and squash are tender.

Shopping list

Oil – 1 tbsp
Onion – 1 small, chopped
Ginger root – 1 inch of, chopped
Garlic – 1 clove, chopped
Fenugreek seeds* – pinch of
Red lentils – 1 cup (200g; 7oz), dry
Butternut squash – ½ a small one, peeled, deseeded and cubed
Coriander – ⅓ cup (40g; 1½ oz), fresh, finely chopped
Water – 2 cups (500ml; 1 pint)
Coconut milk – ¾ cup (185ml; ¼ pint and 4 tbsp)
Tomato purée – 2 tbsp
Curry powder – 1 tsp
Cayenne pepper – 1 pinch
Ground nutmeg – 1 pinch
Salt and pepper – to taste

*Please note: fenugreek seeds are not recommended during pregnancy.

Coconut & Peanut Veggie Sauté

DINNER

30 mins

4 portions

> I lived in Thailand for a year before I went to university. This is not a Thai dish, but it is inspired by the amazing flavours I experienced during my time there. I love coconut in savoury dishes, and this has delicate but memorable flavours that will tickle any little taste bud.

1 In a wok or frying pan, put the oil, garlic, lemon juice and tamari or Liquid Aminos and sauté the onion for one or two minutes.

2 Add the rest of the chopped vegetables and stir until cooked but still crunchy.

3 Mix the sauce ingredients together and pour over the vegetables.

4 Stir until the vegetables are well coated and hot throughout.

5 Serve with rice.

Shopping list

Groundnut (vegetable) oil – splash of
Garlic – 2 large cloves, minced or crushed
Lemon – juice of 1
Tamari (Bragg Liquid Aminos) – 1 tbsp
Red onion – 1 small, sliced
Red bell pepper – 1 large
Broccoli – 1 small head or ½ a large one, chopped
Carrot – 1 small, chopped
Mushrooms – 12 medium, sliced
Baby corn – 1 400g (14 oz) tin

For the sauce:
Coconut milk (light) – 1 cup (250ml; ½ pint)
Peanut butter – 2 tbsp
Tamari (Bragg Liquid Aminos) – ½ tbsp
Chilli flakes – sprinkle of
Cayenne pepper – pinch of (leave this out if you're not into spicy foods)
Ginger – ½ to1-inch piece, peeled and minced or grated

Chickpea Loaf

DINNER

130 mins

2 portions

When I first gave up meat I was a teenager and the only non-meat eater in my family at the time. A nice lady from my church called Linda took me under her wing and taught me how to cook meat-free meals. This is my version of the dish that she taught me. Feel free to experiment and add your favourite seasonings to taste.

1 Cook the soaked chickpeas at a low simmer for 50 minutes to an hour, until soft.

2 Drain the chickpeas, then mash them.

3 Preheat the oven to 190°C (375°F; gas mark 5).

4 Heat the oil in a large frying pan and sauté the garlic and onion for five minutes.

5 Add the celery, carrot, tamari, parsley, cumin, turmeric and salt.

6 Sauté until the vegetables are tender.

7 Add the sautéed vegetables to the mashed chickpeas and mix well.

Shopping list

Chickpeas – 2½ cups (500g; 1 lb 2oz), soaked overnight
Vegetable oil – 2 tbsp
Garlic – 2 cloves, minced
Onion – 1, chopped
Celery stalks – 2, chopped
Carrots – 2, finely chopped
Tamari – ¼ cup (60ml; 2 fl oz)
Parsley – 2 tsp, dried
Cumin – 1 tsp, ground
Turmeric – ¼ tsp
Tahini – 3 tbsp
Salt – pinch

8 Add the tahini and give everything another good mix.

9 Transfer the mixture to a large baking tray or two small loaf tins, greased, and bake for 45 minutes.

10 Serve with salad and/or vegetables.

DINNER

40 mins

4 portions

Caribbean-style Casserole

Tropical sunshine meets the UK in this easy-to-follow and tasty dish. This is great to make if you want something quick and easy that your children will enjoy. Growing up in the UK has exposed me to many British dishes. My parents are Jamaican so I had to put a bit of a Jamaican twist on this.

1 Put **vegetables** in a casserole dish – chopped **onion**, **scallions**, sliced **plantain**, **thyme** and diced **potatoes**.

2 Pour **ketchup** with four cups of warm water over the vegetables. Sprinkle with **all-purpose seasoning**.

3 Add **vegan margarine**. Cover the dish.

4 Cook the dish in the oven on 325°F (162°C or gas mark 3) for 30 minutes or until the vegetables are tender.

Serve with rice.

Shopping list

Potatoes – 4, diced
Plantains – 2, sliced
Onions – 2, chopped
All-purpose seasoning – 1 tsp
Ketchup – 4 oz or 110g
Vegan margarine – 2 oz or 50g
Salt – to taste
Carrots – 3
Vegetable oil – for sautéing
Thyme – 2 oz or 50g (fresh or dried)
Scallions or green onions – 2

DINNER

30 mins

4 portions

Garden Veg Stew

Vegetables are so versatile and you can use them in so many ways to make a tasty meal. Use up your vegetables in this simple tasty stew. You can even vary the vegetables you use as long as they take roughly the same time to cook. Many nutritionists encourage people to consume plenty of fruit and vegetables, five or more portions a day often being recommended. Vegetables play an important role in human nutrition, being mostly low in fat and carbohydrates, but high in vitamins, minerals and dietary fibre.

1 Wash and cut vegetables into small pieces, then caramelise in sugar and half of the vegan margarine.

2 Add gungo peas, onion and salt.

3 Add enough water to cover the vegetables and cook for 15 minutes, or until soft.

4 Cream remaining margarine until soft and add cornstarch, then stir in flour, salt and black pepper. Beat until smooth.

5 Drop creamed batter by spoonfuls into simmering vegetables and cook for 5 more minutes.

Serve hot.

Shopping list

Gungo peas (pigeon peas) – 8 oz (225g)
Carrots – 4 oz (110g), diced
Turnips – 4 oz (110g), diced
Onion – 1, chopped
Sugar – 1 tsp
Vegan margarine – 2 lb (900g)
Flour – 6 tbsp
Salt – 1 tsp
Corn starch/corn flour – 4 tbsp
Black pepper – ¼ tsp
Stew pack mix – 1 lb (450g)

30 mins

4 portions

Easy Vegan Mac & 'Cheese'

A culinary revolution has been going on: the mac and cheese revolution. It appears on high-end restaurant menus, stuffed into burgers, teamed up with vegetables, jazzed up with vegan blue cheese and taking on a life of its own. From a popular, economical boxed kid's lunch, this comfort food has morphed into a new designer cuisine.

1 Heat up the cooked pasta in a large saucepan. Add the vegan butter, nutritional yeast, almond milk, and hot sauce. Stir until well combined.

2 Add the tomato and stir. (You can also use cooked sweet potato, or any other vegetable that you want.)

3 Season with salt, pepper and vegan cheese and enjoy!

Shopping list

Wholemeal pasta – 3 cups cooked wholewheat pasta (any type of small pasta shape will work)
Vegan butter – 2 tbsp
Nutritional yeast – ½ cup
Non-dairy milk – ¼ cup
Hot sauce – to taste
Tomato – 1 small, chopped (optional)
Salt and pepper – to taste
Vegan cheese – to taste

10 mins

4 portions

Sunny Salad Mix

A salad is one of the easiest dishes to prepare. Add a nice dressing and you have a real winner of a dish for both young and old. Serve as a main course or a smaller portion as a side dish. Can be chilled or eaten at room temperature.

1 Rinse **almonds** and **pumpkin seeds**.

2 Place almonds, pumpkin seeds, **diced bell pepper** and **carrot** in a bowl and set aside.

3 Blend **mango**, **paprika**, **salt** and **pepper** in ½ cup water until smooth.

4 Pour over mixture, combine and serve.

Shopping list

Almonds – ½ cup (soaked overnight)
Pumpkin seeds – ½ cup (soaked overnight)
Yellow bell pepper – 1 (diced)
Carrot – 1 (julienned)
Mango – ½ of one
Paprika – ½ tsp
Salt and pepper – to taste

80 mins

4-6 portions

Curried Chickpea & Sweet Potato Pie

1   Place mixing bowl in fridge for 10-15 minutes or until chilled.

2   Preheat oven to 180°C (350°F; gas mark 4).

3   Place flour and curry powder in the chilled mixing bowl.

4   Add butter and vegetable fat and blend until the mixture looks like fine breadcrumbs.

5   Add the cold water slowly (you may not need all of the water).

6   Combine until the mixture forms a dough.

7   Wrap in cling film (or a plastic freezer bag) and place in fridge for at least 30 minutes.

8   Fry onion in the coconut oil.

9   Add garlic, season-all and curry powder.

10   Cook for 4-5 minutes.

11   Add chickpeas, sweet potato and coconut cream.

12   Allow to simmer for 7-10 minutes.

13   Remove pastry from fridge and roll out on a floured surface.

14   Using a pastry cutter, cut out the pastry for the bottom of the pie and place in small pie tins.

15   Add filling.

16   Cut out pastry for the top of the pie.

17   Place pastry on the pie and prick the pie in the middle with a fork.

18   Bake for 20-30 minutes.

19   Allow to cool on a wire rack.

Shopping list

Pastry

Flour – 1 ⅔ cups, plain, unbleached
Salt – ½ tsp
Vegetable fat (Trex) – ⅓ cup
Vegan butter (Vitalite) – ⅓ cup
Water – 250ml, very cold
Mild curry powder – 2 tbsp

Filling

Chickpeas – 1 cup, cooked
Sweet potato – 1 small, peeled and cooked
Onion – 1 small
Curry powder – 2 tsp
Coconut cream – 2-3 oz
Garlic – 1 clove, finely chopped
Tomato purée – 2 tbsp
Coconut oil or virgin olive oil – 1 tbsp
Season-all or garam masala – 1 tbsp

Beany Balls

95 mins

4-6 portions

When I first came across aduki (adzuki) beans, I was not sure what to make with them that would be tasty — but you are going to love these savoury balls of goodness that are delicately seasoned and can be served with rice, spaghetti or steamed vegetables.

1 Preheat oven to 180°C (350°F; gas mark 4).

2 Cook the adzuki beans in boiling water for 40 minutes until tender. Drain and rinse. Let cool.

3 Cook the bulgur wheat in the stock for 10 minutes until the stock is absorbed. Set aside.

4 Heat 1 tbsp olive oil in a skillet to fry onion, garlic, and spices for 4-5 minutes.

5 In a bowl, mix onion, beans, coriander, seasoning, and eggs and mash with a potato masher. Add the breadcrumbs and bulgur wheat and stir well. Cover and chill for 1 hour, or until firm.

6 With wet hands, mould the mixture into 30 ball shapes.

7 Place on a greased baking sheet and bake for 30-40 minutes.

Shopping list

Adzuki beans – 6 oz, soaked overnight
Bulgur wheat – 1⅓ cups
Vegetable stock – 2 cups
Olive oil – 3 tbsp
Onion – 1, finely chopped
Cloves – 2 whole, crushed
Coriander – 1 tsp, ground
Cumin – 1 tsp, ground
Egg replacer – 3 tbsp
Breadcrumbs – ¾ to 1 cup, dried
Curry powder – 2 tbsp, mild

40 mins

3 portions

Vegan Bibimbap

Bibimbap is great for using up extra veggies knocking around your kitchen. Don't be shy to throw in other ingredients and try different combinations served with a good dollop of spicy bibimbap sauce (available at most good Chinese supermarkets); I'm including a non-spicy version here, but feel free to add your favourite hot sauce in it for some extra heat.

1 In a large frying pan, heat 1 tsp sesame oil, and add the julienned carrot, 1 tbsp water, and a pinch of salt. Stir constantly until al dente. Set aside.

2 Follow step 1 with each of the remaining ingredients (apart from the bean sprouts and spinach).

3 Add the bean sprouts to boiling water for 2-3 minutes, drain well, and then season with a drizzle of sesame oil and a pinch of salt. Repeat with the spinach, boiling for around 30 seconds.

4 Put some rice into a bowl, arrange the veggies on top, pop a dollop of sauce in the middle, and sprinkle some sesame seeds on the top. Mix well before eating.

Shopping list

Rice – 3 cups, cooked
Cucumber – ½ cup, julienned
Carrot – ½ cup, julienned
Courgette – ½ cup, julienned
Mushrooms – ½ cup, chopped
Spinach – 1 cup, chopped
Bean sprouts – ½ cup
Sesame oil – 2 tbsp
Salt – pinch

Sauce
Ketchup – ¼ cup
Garlic – 1 clove, minced
Sesame seeds – 1 tbsp

For the sauce:

1 Combine all the ingredients and mix well.

Use the time while preparing the toppings to cook the rice.

SIDE DISHES

Side dishes are a great way to enhance a meal. You can have as few or as many as you like. When I have guests over for dinner I usually make a basic dish of some kind of veggie stew with rice and then have a wide selection of side dishes so that my guests can pick and mix whatever else they would like to have. This is especially great for children so that they can feel more involved in their meal choices.

   I usually make a basic pasta dish for children who are not used to eating a wide variety of foods; so I usually just add a simple tomato-based pasta sauce, and that is usually great for any fussy little eater.

Rainbow Salad

10 mins

4-6 portions

'Eat a rainbow', as the saying goes. Colourful plates are appealing to everyone, especially children. Making a meal colourful is a good way to encourage children to eat more vegetables. A rainbow plate can help you towards eating your five-a-day (five portions of fruit and vegetables). You are also more likely to enjoy eating a colourful and attractive meal.

1 Combine carrot, tomatoes, cabbage, bell peppers, cucumber and pumpkin seeds.

2 In a separate bowl (a small one) mix together the lemon juice, olive oil, salt and pepper.

3 Pour dressing over the salad and mix.

4 Add beetroot.

5 Serve.

Shopping list

Carrot – 1 small, shredded
Cherry tomatoes – 2 cups
Purple cabbage – ¼ cup finely shredded
Bell peppers – 2 small (1 yellow, 1 red), thinly sliced
Cucumber – 1, thinly sliced
Pumpkin seeds – ¼ cup
Beetroot – ½ cup, chopped

Dressing
Lemon – juice of 1
Olive oil – 1 tsp
Salt and pepper – to taste

40 mins

4-6 portions

Butterbean and Potato Mash with Leeks and Dill

Butterbeans are a tasty addition to mashed potatoes. This delicious combination adds more nutrients to the dish and helps children eat a more nutritious and filling meal. In addition, this dish is low in cost but high in nutritional value. Great served with vegan sausages and gravy

1 Put the potatoes in a saucepan, cover with cold water, add the salt and bring to the boil. Cover and leave to simmer until cooked.

2 Sauté the onion, leek and garlic in a frying pan until they are soft. Add the dill and turmeric and stir.

3 Drain the cooked potatoes and mash thoroughly in a large bowl with the butterbeans. Add the contents of the frying pan and mix thoroughly.

4 Grease a deep oven-proof dish with the margarine and pile the mixture in, pressing it down with a fork.

5 Bake in a hot oven for 15-20 minutes.

Shopping list

Butterbeans – 14 oz (400g), cooked
Potatoes – 1½ pounds, peeled and cubed
Onion – 1, chopped
Garlic – 3 cloves, crushed
Leek – 1, finely chopped
Dill – handful of fresh, finely chopped
Margarine – 1 oz (25g), plus extra for greasing the oven dish
Turmeric – 1 heaped tsp, ground
Salt – 1 level tsp

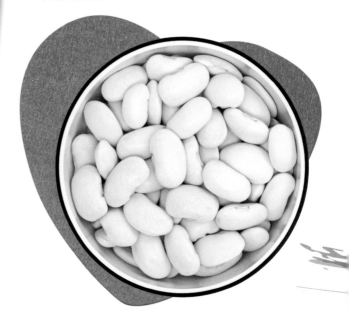

Hummus

20 mins

4-6 portions

Vegans sometimes struggle to find nice side dishes, salad dips and sandwich fillers. Hummus is the vegan answer to all of those things. You can use it for all of those. As a side dish it can be served with some nice toasted pitta bread slices. Serve with a salad or use it to make a sandwich with some raw grated carrot.

1 Drain chickpeas, reserving ¼ cup of liquid.

2 Combine remaining ingredients in blender or food processor.

3 Add reserved ¼ cup of liquid from chickpeas.

4 Blend for 3-5 minutes on low until thoroughly mixed and smooth.

5 Place in serving bowl, and create a shallow well in the centre of the hummus.

6 Add a small amount (1-2 tablespoons) of olive oil in the well.

7 Garnish with parsley or coriander (optional).

Shopping list

Chickpeas – 16 oz, cooked
Lemon juice – 3-5 tbsp (or to taste)
Tahini – 1½ tbsp
Garlic – 2 cloves, crushed
Salt – ½ tsp
Olive oil – 2 tbsp

Baked Potato Stars & Squares

Presentation can make any meal look much more attractive, so what better way to encourage your little ones than to make the food into really attractive shapes? Everyone loves stars, and squares are easy to form; so get creative with your shapes, using small cookie cutters to help you.

40 mins

4-6 portions

1 Preheat oven to 180°C (350°F; gas mark 4).

2 Peel and slice potatoes into thick slices (about ½ inch to 1 inch thick).

3 Parboil potatoes with the crushed garlic on medium heat for 7-10 minutes.

4 Drain potatoes.

5 Spread the potato slices out on a flat surface.

6 Use a small cookie cutter to make the star shapes and you can use a knife to cut out the square shapes.

7 Place the cut-out potatoes onto a greased baking sheet.

8 Bake for 15-20 minutes, or until golden brown and soft inside.

9 Sprinkle with salt and pepper to taste.

Shopping list

Potatoes – 2 lb
Olive oil – drizzle
Garlic – 3 cloves, crushed
Salt and pepper – to taste

40 mins

2 portions

Sweet Potato Fries

This is a great healthy alternative to regular fries. They can be oven-baked or deep-fried. I prefer oven-baked as it's less oily and a healthier way to cook. This is good if you are trying to reduce a few calories for your child if they have a weight issue.

1 Preheat the oven to 240°C (475°F; gas mark 9).

2 Peel the potatoes and slice lengthwise into rectangular fries.

3 Bring a large saucepan of salted water to the boil.

4 Add the fries and cook for 8-10 minutes.

5 Drain and leave to dry for 10 minutes.

6 Grease a baking tray with spray oil.

7 Place the fries on the tray, and spray lightly with spray oil.

8 Bake in the oven for 20-25 minutes, turning occasionally, until golden brown on all sides.

Shopping list

Sweet potatoes – 900g (2 lb) medium-sized
Spray oil
Water
Salt

Sweetcorn Salad

183 mins

4-6 portions

I love to make a salad because it's one of the easiest dishes to make, and you don't need to be a culinary genius to make one either. This is a great dish that children can help to prepare, and it helps them to start on their journey of healthy eating.

1 Combine sweetcorn, carrot, bell peppers, onions and cucumber.

2 Add the dressing and toss the salad lightly. Refrigerate 1-3 hours.

3 Drain and toss the salad lightly before serving.

Vegan Salad Dressing:
(makes ¼ pint or 125ml)

1 Stir all ingredients together.

Shopping list

Sweetcorn – 1 lb and 1 oz (500g), cooked
Carrot – ½ oz (10g), shredded
Green bell peppers – 3 oz (75g), chopped
Spring onions – 1 tbsp, finely chopped
Cucumber – 1 oz (25g), diced

Dressing
Brown sugar – 1 tbsp
Lemon juice – 2-3 tbsp
Spring onion – 1 sprig, finely chopped
Light olive oil – 1-2 tbsp

Crunchy Coleslaw

30 mins

6-8 portions

The word 'coleslaw' comes from the Dutch word 'koolsla', which means cabbage salad. I am not a great fan of cabbage, but mix it in a coleslaw and I can eat lots of it. I think many people feel the same, and children will be no exception. Dress up the good food in an appealing way and most children will eat it.

1 Combine cabbage, carrots, bell pepper, onions and mayonnaise. Chill well.

2 Just before serving, combine oil and vinegar. Mix well.

3 Pour over chilled vegetables and mix lightly.

Shopping list

Vegan mayonnaise – 2 oz (50g)
Cabbage – 5 oz (150g), shredded
Carrots – 1 oz (25g), shredded
Green bell pepper – 1½ oz (40g), finely chopped
Onions – 1½ oz (40g), finely chopped
Olive oil – ¼ pint (125ml)
Apple cider vinegar – to taste

Vegan snacks are just as varied and exciting as any other kind of snacks. I find them particularly useful when travelling overseas. Fruits make great snacks, as they are all vegan and many come in handy portion sizes already. Berries are great too: just put 1-2 handfuls into a plastic container and there is your snack. I love a mixture of nuts, dried fruits and seeds, as these can be made in advance and then you can just grab and go when you need them. Get your little ones to create their favourite combinations of dried fruits, nuts and seeds.

Snacks can also be quite unhealthy, so keep an eye on the salt and sugar content. The amount of snacks eaten is important too. Small, healthy snacks are OK, but if you have too many it becomes an extra meal instead of just a small snack.

40 mins

6 portions

Coconut Chips

It's very easy to buy a packet of crisps (or chips as they call them in some countries). They are usually not very healthy, but children adore them. What better way to wean your children from crisps than by making homemade ones instead?

1 Toast coconut in a moderate oven (180°C; 350°F; gas mark 4) for about 10 minutes.

2 Keep stirring to even the cooking. Remove from oven and allow to cool.

3 Sieve flour and baking powder together.

4 Melt margarine and mix in.

5 Add coconut and coconut milk, and mix to a smooth paste.

6 Turn out onto a well-floured board.

7 Roll thinly and cut into desired shapes.

8 Place on a greased baking tray and bake in a moderate oven (350°F, 180°C or gas mark 4) for about 20 minutes.

Shopping list

Coconut – 6 oz (175g), grated (remove brown coating)
Flour – 5 oz (150g)
Baking powder – 1 tsp
Vegan margarine – 2 tbsp
Coconut milk – ¼ pint (125ml)

180 mins

6-8 portions

No-bake Granola Bars

Granola bars are so fun to make. The recipe is easy, and this one doesn't even require an oven. If you want to try out a few raw vegan recipes on your children then this is a good one to start with. Packed with lots of healthy goodness, you can get creative and use this as a basis to create other flavours or versions too.

1 Line a medium-sized shallow baking tray, about 20x30cm, with greaseproof paper.

2 Put the dates, bananas, agave (or maple) syrup, coconut oil and 2 tablespoons water in a food processor and blend.

3 In a large bowl, combine the oats, raisins, currants, flaxseed, sunflower seeds and pumpkin seeds.

4 Stir in the puréed fruit and agave, and mix well.

5 Place the mixture into the prepared tin and gently press it down, getting it as even and level as you can.

6 Put the tray in the fridge for 2-3 hours to allow the flapjack to set, and then turn out onto a board and slice into bars.

7 Keep in a plastic container in the fridge and eat within a week.

Shopping list

Dates – 200g, pitted
Bananas – 2, slightly over-ripe
Agave or maple syrup – 150g
Coconut oil – 2 tbsp, raw organic
Oats – 325g, porridge or jumbo
Raisins – 100g
Currants – 50g
Flaxseed (linseed) – 25g
Sunflower seeds – 25g
Pumpkin seeds – 30g
Water – 2 tbsp

Fruity Trail Mix

SNACKS

5 mins

2 portions

I have a busy schedule, and when you are on the go it is good to have something that you can make ahead of time that you can just grab and go. Especially on the days when you have woken up late or haven't done any meal prep, this is great recipe. I also find this handy when I am travelling. I always take snacks with me on flights so that I have something nutritious and vegan-friendly that I can enjoy

1 Place all ingredients in a large bowl.

2 Mix well.

3 Store in a plastic bag or glass jar.

This will keep for up to one month.

Shopping list

Pecans – ½ cup, chopped
Cashews – ½ cup, chopped
Almonds – ½ cup, chopped
Pumpkin seeds – ½ cup
Sunflower seeds – ½ cup
Raisins – ½ cup
Sultanas – ½ cup
Cranberries – ½ cup, dried (or other berries)
Sea salt – ¼ tsp
Cinnamon – ½ tsp
Nutmeg – ¼ tsp

10 mins

5-7 portions

Bugs on a Log

Could this recipe be any more cute? Children love these tasty treats that resemble nature's cute little bugs on a log. This is a great recipe that children can make, and is great for parties or if you have little guests coming to visit.

1 Chop each celery stick into 2 or 3 even lengths.

2 Evenly fill the hollows of the celery with peanut butter.

3 Place a line of raisins along the length of the celery stick on top of the peanut butter.

4 Serve.

Shopping list

Celery – 5-7 sticks
Peanut butter – ½ cup, smooth
Raisins – ¼ cup

40 mins

12 portions

Peanut Butter & Banana Flapjacks

I created this recipe because I love flapjacks. However, when you try to buy them in the UK the majority are not vegan-friendly, so I decided to make my own. The topping was a suggestion from my cousin Sherna, who was at my house one day when I was making them and suggested that I give them a topping. I liked her suggestion and changed my recipe to include it, so I now always make it with a topping.

1 Preheat oven to 160°C (140°C with fan; gas mark 3).

2 Grease and line a 20cm square tin with baking parchment.

3 Heat the butter, peanut butter and maple syrup in a small pan until melted.

4 Add the mashed banana, apple and 100ml hot water, and mix to combine.

5 Tip the oats, the raisins and the seeds into a large bowl.

6 Pour in the combined banana and apple and stir until everything is coated by the wet mixture.

7 Tip into the cake tin and level the surface.

8 Combine topping ingredients together in a blender and sprinkle evenly on top.

9 Bake for 55 mins until golden.

10 Leave to cool in the tin.

11 Cut into 12 pieces to serve (or store in an airtight container in the fridge).

Shopping list

Vegan butter – 50g, plus a little extra for greasing
Peanut butter – 2 tbsp, smooth
Maple syrup or agave syrup – 3 tbsp
Bananas – 2, ripe, mashed
Apple – 1, peeled and grated
Rolled oats – 250g
Raisins – 100g
Seeds – 85g, mixed (pumpkin and sunflower)

Topping
Almonds – 50g
Brown sugar – 50g
Cinnamon – ¼ tsp

SNACKS

50 mins

6-8 portions

Baked Chickpeas

Chickpeas (garbanzo beans) are one of my store cupboard staples. I use chickpeas for so many different dishes. According to Wikipedia, chickpeas are a nutrient-dense food, providing a rich content (20% or higher of the Daily Value, DV) of protein, dietary fibre, folate, and certain dietary minerals such as iron and phosphorus. This makes baked chickpeas a perfect savoury snack for children.

1 Preheat oven to 450°F (230°C).

2 Blot chickpeas with a paper towel to dry them.

3 In a bowl, mix chickpeas with olive oil.

4 Stir in the salt, garlic granules, onion granules and mixed herbs.

5 Spread out in an even layer on a baking sheet.

6 Bake for 30 to 40 minutes, or until browned and slightly crunchy.

Shopping list

Chickpeas – 12 oz, cooked
Olive oil – 2 tbsp
Salt – ¼ tsp
Garlic salt – ½ tsp
Onion salt – ½ tsp
Mixed herbs – 1 tsp

40 mins

5 portions

Vegan Rice Rolls

These colourful rolls are easier than you think, and look great! I've included Korean pickled radish for extra crunch, but don't worry if you can't get any: just leave it out. These can be tailor-made with your favourite vegetables.

1. In a large frying pan heat 1 tsp sesame oil and add the julienned carrot, 1 tbsp water, and a pinch of salt. Stir constantly until al dente. Set aside.

2. Follow step 1 with each of the remaining ingredients (apart from the spinach and Korean pickled radish).

3. Add the spinach to boiling water for 30 seconds to wilt, drain well, and then season with a drizzle of sesame oil and a pinch of salt.

4. On a bamboo mat, cover a sheet of nori with a ½-inch layer of rice – leaving an inch at the top edge.

5. Place the radish strip and vegetables in packed lines towards the bottom edge of the rice.

6. Carefully roll the mat from the bottom edge up, keeping your vegetables tucked inside. Give your rolled mat a squeeze before unrolling.

7. Repeat with all your nori sheets, and then cut each into inch-wide sections. Serve with sweet chilli sauce.

Shopping list

Nori sheets – 1 packet (5 sheets)
Carrot – ½ cup, julienned
Cucumber – ½ cup, julienned
Spinach – 1 cup, chopped
Pepper – ½ cup, julienned
Sushi rice – 2 cups, cooked
Korean pickled radish – 5 (optional)
Sesame oil – 2 tbsp
Salt – pinch

Bamboo mats are tricky to wash – so skip this step by wrapping your mat generously in cling film first.

CAKES, BAKES & DESSERTS

So who doesn't love dessert? I know that some people say they are not dessert people and I always joke that there should be a helpline for that. I LOVE desserts; I have a sweet tooth. I do try to monitor my sugar intake to keep it fairly low. Desserts can be a delight and not a sugar overload if you are keeping an eye on the amount of sugar you consume.

Be careful with the sugar alternatives as some are no better than processed sugar. The best alternative is to use natural unprocessed sugar, or just to use less sugar. A dessert with lots of fruit is good, but it can be an overly predictable vegan dessert option. Instead you could roast/bake the fruit with cinnamon and vanilla and serve with vegan cream or ice cream.

15 mins

4 portions

Chocolate Mousse

There is the misconception that when you become a vegan you miss out on great desserts. . . . Wrong. There are many lip-smacking vegan desserts that you can make. Like thousands of people across the globe, I am a lover of chocolate. Vegan chocolate mousse is such a joy to make as it has a wonderful chocolate flavour. Try serving this with fresh raspberries or strawberries or whatever fruit you have locally that goes with chocolate.

1 Peel and then mash the flesh of the avocados with a fork.

2 Add in cocoa powder, agave nectar, vanilla and almond extract and blend for 1 to 2 minutes, making sure every part is well blended.

3 Refrigerate overnight and serve.

Shopping list

Avocados – 2 large, ripe
Cocoa powder – ½ cup unsweetened
Agave nectar or maple syrup – ½ cup
Vanilla – 1½ tsp
Almond extract or almond milk – 1½ tsp

65 mins

6-8 portions

Banana Cake

I used to make this banana cake for a health food shop in North London. I would bake multiple loaves of it and sell it to the shop, and they would then sell it by the slice. They always sold out really quickly, and no matter how many loaves I made they would always sell out. I think that is why I've decided to include this recipe in this book, as I know it is well loved by both young and old.

1 Preheat oven to 190ºC (375ºF; gas mark 5).

2 Mix together all ingredients until combined.

3 Pour mixture into a medium-sized cake tin, greased and lined with greaseproof paper.

4 Bake for 55 minutes, or until a toothpick placed in the middle comes out clean.

5 Allow to cool and then serve.

Shopping list

Bananas – 1 lb (450g), ripe, mashed
Light flavourless oil – 4 oz (100ml):
for example, sunflower
Raisins – 4 oz (100g)
Rolled oats – 3 oz (75g)
Wholewheat or spelt flour – 5 oz (150g)
Cinnamon – ¼ tsp
Nutmeg – ¼ tsp
Pinch of salt

32 mins

8 portions

Pumpkin & Raisin Cupcakes

As a child I did not like pumpkin. Even when I tried to smother it with butter (which was not encouraged by my parents) I still had to force it down. When I became an adult I travelled to the USA many times on business trips and discovered that Americans use pumpkin to make desserts. I was a bit hesitant to try it at first, but now I am a fan.

1 Preheat oven to 180°C (350°F).

2 Line a muffin tin with cupcake cases.

3 In a medium mixing bowl mix together the cooked pumpkin, canola oil, soya milk, sugar and vanilla.

4 When this is thoroughly mixed, sift in the flour, baking powder, baking soda, cinnamon and salt. Use a fork or whisk, not an electric mixer, to mix the dry ingredients in.

5 When thoroughly mixed, pour in the raisins and stir well.

6 Pour mixture into the cupcake cases, filling each space about two-thirds full. (The cupcakes will rise quite a lot, so don't overfill the cupcake cases.)

7 Bake for approximately 22 minutes, or until a toothpick placed in the centre comes out clean.

Shopping list

Pumpkin – 2 cups, cooked
Flour – 2½ cups
Granulated sugar – 2 cups
Raisins – 1 cup
Canola oil (or rapeseed or olive) – ⅔ cup
Almond (or rice) milk – ½ cup
Vanilla extract – 2 tsp
Baking powder – 1 tsp
Baking soda – 1 tsp
Ground cinnamon – 1 tsp
Pinch of salt

158

32 mins

4-6 portions

Pineapple & Banana Pudding

I discovered pineapple pudding from one of my American friends called Nicki whom I met when I lived overseas. This is my version of the dish she showed me how to make. It is a nice healthy dessert that can be adapted to include any of your favourite fruits that pair well with pineapple.

1 Place pineapple juice, cornstarch and 2 bananas in a blender and blend until smooth.

2 Transfer mixture to a pot and cook on medium heat until thickened, stirring constantly.

3 Remove from heat, add crushed pineapple and stir.

4 Pour over the remaining 2 sliced bananas in dessert dishes.

 Shopping list

Pineapple juice – 1¼ pints (625ml), unsweetened
Cornstarch – 5 tsp
Bananas – 4, peeled and chopped
Pineapple – 8 oz (225g) crushed, fresh (if using tinned pineapple use natural juice from the tin and omit unsweetened pineapple juice above)

120 mins

8 portions

Dairy-free Strawberry & Banana Ice Cream

Ice cream is a global treat that is enjoyed by both young and old. If this is your first time making non-dairy ice cream, you will be amazed to see that this has a very similar texture to regular ice cream. You can vary this recipe and make almost any flavour, including chocolate.

1 Freeze strawberries and bananas for at least two hours or overnight.

2 Soak dates in enough water to cover them, until soft – once soft, drain off the water.

3 Put the frozen strawberries and bananas into a food processor.

4 Add the vanilla extract and dates.

5 Blend until smooth and creamy.

Shopping list

Strawberries – 1 punnet, hulled and frozen
Bananas – 3, peeled, chopped and frozen
Dates – 5-6, medjool or ordinary
Vanilla extract – 1 tsp (or pod)

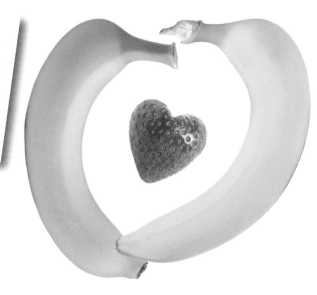

40 mins

2 portions

Almond & Raisin Cake

I have times when I feel like a cake-a-holic (if there is such a thing). I love to bake, and this is one of my go-to recipes when I feel the need to bake a cake. I've made this cake for my non-vegan friends who had no clue that it was made with no dairy or eggs but soon realised that it's the only way I would make it. They enjoyed it and came back for more.

1 Preheat oven to 190ºC (375ºF; gas mark 5).

2 Place wholemeal flour, baking powder, ground almonds, egg replacer and raisins in a bowl and stir.

3 In a separate bowl mix together the milk and maple syrup.

4 Gradually add the milk mixture to the dry ingredients and stir well.

5 Bake in greased cake tin for 45-60 minutes, or until a knife inserted in the middle comes out fairly clean.

6 Cool before serving.

7 This cake can be sliced and served with butter (you can use dairy-free butter if desired).

Shopping list

Wholemeal flour – 1 cup
Baking powder – 2 tsp
Almonds – 1 cup, ground
Raisins (or chopped, soaked dates) – 1 cup
Almond milk – 1 cup
Egg replacer – 1 heaped tsp
Maple syrup or honey – 1 tbsp

60 mins

6-8 portions

Vegan Orchard Fruit Crumble

As a child I grew up eating apple crumble at school. They also served rhubarb crumble, but I'm not a fan of rhubarb. I decided to make apple crumble with a twist. Using some of my favourite orchard fruits gives it a much richer flavour that is surprising with each spoonful, as you never know which fruit you will bite into next.

1 Preheat the oven to 170°C.

2 In a saucepan, over a gentle-to-moderate heat, cook all the fruits in the water until soft and stewed. Keep stirring to prevent fruits from sticking and burning on bottom of pan. It cooks more quickly if, in between stirring, you keep the lid on too.

3 Meanwhile, in a mixing bowl, rub the margarine and flour with your fingertips until it completely blends together and you get a fine crumble.

4 Add the ground almonds, 2 tbsp of the sugar and the nutmeg, and stir the mixture well.

5 When the apples have stewed, add the leftover tbsp of the sugar and the cinnamon and cloves and stir in until sugar dissolves.

6 Put the fruit mixture in an ovenproof dish and cover with the crumble.

7 Bake for approximately half an hour, or until the crumble is golden brown.

Shopping list

Apple – 1, chopped into small pieces
Pear – 1, chopped into small pieces
Blackberries – ½ cup
Raspberries – ½ cup
Water – 5 tbsp
Wholemeal flour – 4 tbsp
Vegan margarine – 1 tbsp
Brown sugar – 3 tbsp
Cinnamon – 1 tsp
Nutmeg – ½ tsp
Cloves – ¼ tsp
Almonds – 1 cup, ground

40 mins

6 portions

Scones

Scones are traditionally served with butter or with jam and cream. In the UK you can be served a meal called 'tea' and many high-end restaurants will have this option. For children this is great, as it is easy to make and you can add raisins if you so desire. I have made these as a special treat when I have little guests come to visit.

1 Preheat the oven to 220°C (425°F; gas mark 7).

2 Sift the flour and baking powder into a large bowl, and rub in the non-dairy margarine until the mixture resembles breadcrumbs.

3 Add the sugar and mix together thoroughly.

4 Make a well in the middle of the mixture, and slowly pour in the non-dairy milk, stirring with a metal spoon. Add the dried fruit. Bring the mixture together until it forms a dough.

5 Generously flour a large board and knead the dough for five minutes. Roll it out to a thickness of about 2.5cm (1 inch) and, using a fluted 9cm (3-inch) cutter, cut rounds from the dough.

6 Place the rounds on a greased and floured non-stick baking tray, and glaze the top using the extra non-dairy milk.

7 Bake in the top of the oven for about 15 minutes, or until a deep golden brown colour.

8 Leave to cool.

9 Serve with strawberry jam.

Shopping list

Self-raising flour – 8 oz
Baking powder – 1 tsp
Non-dairy margarine – 1½ oz, plus extra for greasing
Caster sugar – 2 tbsp
Non-dairy milk – 150ml (4¼ fl oz), plus extra for glazing
Dried fruit – 4 oz (such as raisins)

JUICES & SMOOTHIES

I love smoothies! I think they are a great way to consume more fruits and vegetables. I had some friends over for a girly sleepover once. I decided to create a smoothie bar for them. I washed and chopped the fruits and placed them in containers. I had non-dairy milk, orange juice and water for blending. I also had tall glasses and straws for serving. Each person got to pick and blend their own combination of fruits to create their own smoothie.

The result was that my guests loved it, and I also tried this when I had some of my young relatives come to stay — and they loved it too! Try this out with your children. This is a good idea for a children's party because it will be fun and a good healthy option too.

Green Juice

3 apples

3 kale leaves

2 sticks celery

1 cucumber

Sweet Beet Juice

1 small, uncooked sweet potato
(peeled)

1 small beetroot

2 apples

Handful raspberries

2-3 plums (pitted)

Bunny's
Favourite Juice

4-6 carrots

2 apples

Juice all the ingredients in a juicer.
Drink immediately, or let it chill
for an hour and then enjoy

Cool Juice

1 cucumber

2-3 apples

Jungle Juice

½ small pineapple

1 orange

1 lemon

¼ coconut

Tree Fruit Juice

1 orange

2-3 apples

1 pear

Juice all the ingredients in a juicer. Drink immediately, or let it chill for an hour and then enjoy

Pineapple & Banana Smoothie

2 cups pineapple

2 ripe bananas

1 tbsp maple syrup

1 cup rice milk or almond milk

Sunshine Smoothie

1 medium mango

1 handful pineapple pieces

1 banana

1 kiwi

1 orange

1 tbsp maple syrup

1 cup water

Strawberry & Banana Smoothie

2 cups strawberries

2 ripe bananas

1 tbsp maple syrup

1 cup rice milk or almond milk

Place the ingredients in a blender. Blend until smooth.

Super Hero Smoothie

1 kale leaf (chopped)

2 apples
(cored and chopped)

1 banana (chopped)

1 stick celery

½ cucumber

1 tbsp maple syrup

1 cup water

Princess Pink Smoothie

1 apple

1-2-inch piece beetroot

1 tbsp maple syrup

1 handful strawberries

1 pear

1 cup water

Man-apple -berry Smoothie

1 medium ripe mango

1 apple

1 tbsp maple syrup

1 handful raspberries

1 cup water

Place the ingredients in a blender.
Blend until smooth.

Index

Eating for Life

Clemency Mitchell

Additional contributors: Lucinda Annan,
Agnes David, Angeline Francis, Huldah Or...
and Thelma Soremekun

Juicing for Life

by Beverley Ramages